WORD ON THE STREET

"Jim Knight is a rock star writer and observer of talent like the many music agents and producers I work with on a regular basis. His unique observations of top talent become a textbook for the highest-level service in any industry. Like a concert that fires on all cylinders, *Service That Rocks* leaves a lasting memory that, well, really rocks!"

Michael Dorf, City Winery, founder & chairman

"We all know the danger of producing sequels: they don't always live up to the original. But in *Service That Rocks*, my good friend Jim Knight does what Hollywood often fails to do—he exceeds the standard previously set. Jim's first book, *Culture That Rocks*, is easily one of my favorites in the organization-building space. In his third book, he goes deeper into customer service. Grab your highlighter because this one is filled with nuggets!"

Don Yaeger, certified speaking professional, eleven-time bestselling author, executive coach

"Florida's hospitality industry lives and dies by the customer experience and the service we provide our guests. Jim Knight's newest book, *Service That Rocks*, is the perfect business blueprint to help your establishment surpass guest expectations and keep them coming back for more. There are so many incredible takeaways in this book for employees and leaders alike; it is a must-read. Just like Jim, this book rocks!"

Carol Dover, Florida Restaurant and Lodging Association, president & CEO

"In *Service That Rocks*, Jim Knight delivers practical insight, incredible stories and a game plan for delivering a brand experience that will keep customers coming back for more. This book is an entertaining read packed with actionable ideas to influence culture, inspire employees and deliver a service experience that surprises and delights every single time. When it comes to the future of customer experience, I learn from Jim, and if you care about your customers, I cannot recommend this book enough!"

Ryan Estis, keynote speaker, author and service training expert

"Jim Knight delivers the ultimate formula for service success in *Service That Rocks* by combining a rock star mentality, innovative techniques and best practices to competitively differentiate your business. Jim has perfected the playlist to engage employees at every level to deliver your organization's service culture and create fans for life in today's dynamic marketplace. Fun, practical and action-oriented—this book has it all!"

Kathleen Wood, speaker, author, executive consultant and CEO of Suzy's Swirl

"At the largest culinary school in the world, we train personnel to work in the biggest service-oriented industry; as the school's CEO, I know relevance and value when I see it. In *Service That Rocks*, Jim Knight delivers thought-provoking wisdom and practical advice for employees to create unforgettable customer experiences, which lead to sustainable and unforgettable brands. This book rocks!"

Tracy Lorenz, Auguste Escoffier School of Culinary Arts, president & CEO

Rock On!

SERVICE
THAT
ROCKS

SERVICE

JIM KNIGHT

CREATE
UNFORGETTABLE
EXPERIENCES AND
TURN CUSTOMERS
INTO FANS

THAT
ROCKS

PAGE TWO

Cataloguing in publication information is
available from Library and Archives Canada.
ISBN 978-1-77458-305-0 (paperback)
ISBN 978-1-77458-306-7 (ebook)

Page Two
pagetwo.com

Edited by Kendra Ward
Copyedited by Jenny Govier
Cover and interior design by Peter Cocking
Printed and bound in Canada

ServiceThatRocksBook.com
KnightSpeaker.com

For my dad, James R. Knight—

my personal mentor and hero to many

SET LIST

SOUND
CHECK

LIVE IN the land of theme parks: Central Florida. Families from around the world spend thousands of dollars and an entire week to come to Orlando with the expectation that they will fully experience the "happiest place on Earth." Walt Disney World, Universal Studios, SeaWorld, Busch Gardens, LEGO-LAND, Gatorland... we have something for everyone.

As a local resident, I am hyperaware that when I go out to eat, drink, shop, stay, play and even travel, I will inevitably see little girls, ages three to four years old, dressed up as princesses. I am not talking about some homemade, handsewn craft attempts that "resemble" Cinderella, Elsa or Snow White, but full-on, professionally produced and expensive outfits, tiaras included. These kids most likely are not dressed up as royalty because their families are going to one of the theme parks. Rather, they just want to channel their inner princesses and wear the outfits as their daily attire of choice. I see these adorable wonders everywhere.

A few years ago, I was in a fast casual restaurant, where I had already put in my to-go order at the counter and had stepped back to await my food. As I was standing there, I watched a "princess" hesitantly approach the counter with a $5 bill in her hand. I knew exactly what was happening, because I could see the little girl's mother over to the side watching her daughter buy her own ice cream cone. As she approached the teenage cashier, he reacted to the little girl as if she were actual royalty by simultaneously bowing, doing a fancy hand flourish and loudly belting out in a British accent, "'Ello there, m'lady!"

It was such a cool moment—especially to see the size of the grin on the child's face—but that is not what rocked my world; it's what the cashier did after his greeting that propelled him to icon status.

He loudly pronounced to everyone within ear shot, "All hail the princess," which prompted every single restaurant team member—the food expediter, other cashiers, the drive-thru host, the fry cook and the manager—to stop what they were doing, turn toward the little girl in unison, bow to her royal highness and then return to what they were previously doing.

I lost my mind.

It was such a mind-searing moment that, even today, I still feel pure joy every time I reflect on it.

As an experience-starved consumer actively on the hunt for moments like this to present themselves, I constantly think back on this experience as a template of what *could be* for service-oriented businesses. What transpired that day is not something that is explicitly taught in this national brand. That specific experience was authentically produced by a keenly aware service rock star on a daily mission to bring extra joy to others' lives. He did this on his own. And somehow he had coerced all of his work buddies to join in on the fun to collectively produce moments that young girls (and their mothers) will remember for the rest of their lives. The interaction only took seconds and it cost nothing... but the experience was unforgettable.

We need more of that in the world.

I am consumed with finding people who deliver experiences like this and companies that foster a culture that allows these moments to exist. Even more so, as a former public middle school teacher and executive training professional and now keynote speaker, sharing experiential best practices—which I call "service that rocks"—has become my obsession.

My sincere desire is to help companies amp up their service practices and create lifelong raving fans. The service philosophy and the techniques used do not have to be as grandiose, over-the-top or mind-blowing as acknowledging little girls dressed up as princesses, but even in the most mundane customer interactions, we can still treat the end user as rock royalty. That is what sustainable brands do to continuously stay relevant in the consumer's mind.

Imagine if every business took on this awesome responsibility with the same vigor, every day, with every customer. You could practically guarantee better results in the areas that matter. Justin Timberlake tells us that what goes around comes around. I believe brands would absolutely be rewarded.

That's how companies become legendary.

Let's help yours do just that.

SUSTAINABLE BRANDS TREAT THE END USER AS ROCK ROYALTY.

———

Anything worth doing
is worth overdoing.

MICK JAGGER

SETTING
THE STAGE

THE TERM "culture" is nebulous, but you likely have a preconceived notion of what company culture is. Perhaps you see it as external: the way others see your brand. Or you might equate culture with your internal environment: the way the employees feel and act. Culture is actually a combination of both, but it always starts internally.

In my first book, *Culture That Rocks: How to Revolutionize a Company's Culture*, I defined company culture as a collection of individual behaviors. That's it. Obviously, much more detail went into why I believe this, but beyond everything else about an organization, the company's soul is made up of human behaviors. Whoever is working in the business at any given time... *that* is the true company culture.

An organization's public "personality" doesn't occur and thrive on its own; it is predicated upon the internal microculture of human beings *making* it come to life. Changing internal employee behaviors, therefore, directly affects the end user's view of the brand's culture. If you seek to change the image projected to the general public, you have to change the way your organization behaves and operates internally.

I'm going to make a leap and assume that the reason you picked up this book is because you are looking to improve your company's execution in a specific area: service. Whatever your industry, you either sell a product or provide a basic service to your consumers, and you think that improving the way your product or service is delivered to others can create the cultural overhaul you seek. And you would be correct. I've, therefore, crafted this book around the topic of "customer service," as this is a key element in positive culture change in many companies.

After all, what's the point of working on all the tactical initiatives required for running the business if the overall crux of the business is in providing a service to others—and *that* part of the brand is broken? Addressing everything but the main function of the organization is like rearranging the deck chairs on the *Titanic*. There may be additional organizational issues to address, but for service-oriented companies, hope for success in other areas of the business only exists when it's anchored by phenomenal customer experiences.

Fix this and, in many companies, the overall culture will flourish.

THE WHY BEHIND THE WHAT

When it comes to the topic of "customer experience," I have a lot to say. My opinions are not unique to the average consumer who just wants to be treated as special during a financial transaction, but I am hypersensitive to what it *could be* because of the two decades I spent working for one of the greatest service-oriented companies on the planet: Hard Rock International. No doubt the time I spent immersed in that authentic, unpredictable and sometimes irreverent hospitality brand helped shape who I am today and my philosophies. But those years were just the catalyst for the customer service content and programs I now share with organizations around the world.

Since I "retired from corporate life," I've had the great fortune to give keynote speeches to fantastic organizations in many different industries and countries. I've studied and spent time with amazing leaders who have taken their brands to iconic heights, and I've written bestselling books on the topics of company culture and leadership. This book is the next evolution, designed to help companies and individuals differentiate themselves from their competitors to achieve long-term sustainability and relevance.

Let me set the stage.

THE SERIES

When I launched *Culture That Rocks* in 2014, I laid out a holistic approach to enhancing a brand. But like trying to explain the meaning of life, the definition of love, the secrets of the universe or why Garth Brooks secretly recorded an album as the alt-rocker Chris Gaines, you can only provide so much information in one place and still produce an interesting, coherent resource.

THE CUSTOMER EXPERIENCE IS CRITICAL TO COMPANY CULTURE.

———

That first book covers a lot of ground, touching on many facets of organizational culture: hiring and retaining top talent, fostering a diverse workforce, delivering stellar customer service, enhancing communication, supporting philanthropy, adopting technology, creating compelling branding and the type of leadership required to make it all happen. Those concepts are like hit songs in a longer playlist of company culture, many with an arc I explore further—and in more detail—in this Culture That Rocks series.

That was the ultimate plan: to deconstruct my first "book baby" into three specific, detailed and relevant books, each with its own heightened message and set of learnings.

Leadership That Rocks was the first book, which laid the groundwork for the others. Now, I present the second book, *Service That Rocks*, which spotlights how critical the customer experience is to creating, maintaining or revolutionizing a company's culture.

Like those that came before it, this book includes ideas, stories and best practices for how to strengthen the service culture of a business. The final act in the three-book series will be *Engagement That Rocks*, which will focus on finding and holding on to the frontline rock stars that every great sustainable brand needs to make it all happen.

Here are the other books in the series:

Leadership That Rocks
Take Your Brand's Culture to Eleven and Amp Up Results

Engagement That Rocks
Recruit and Retain Chart-Topping Talent

You can easily look at each book as a singular, targeted and robust resource addressing a specific need of the business—and that may be the exact solution your company needs to amp up results. But if you collect the entire series, you will be investing in a detailed and holistic blueprint for sustaining your company's culture at legendary heights.

And that will just make you rock even harder.

THE REAL WORK

The real impact will come when you put in the work of studying and implementing my suggestions. In the learning and development world, there is a big difference between a collection of words on a piece of paper and a compelling video, where the visual nuances create much more interest and eventual stickiness. I'm an educator at heart; my hope is that you retain and actively implement the ideas I share with you so that you can create a best-in-class service culture.

At the end of each chapter of this book, I provide an at-a-glance review of its most impactful points. Consider these the main lyrics of the overall tune, so that you don't get lost in the melody and the beat.

In addition to this low-hanging fruit, the "Encore" section at the end of the book includes action items you can do to immediately enhance your customer service approaches and ignite your brand's cultural revolution.

TRUTH BOMB

When you purchased this book, you invested in the future: the future of your career, the future of your business and the future of an integral piece of your company's identity—its service culture. Through thick and thin, good times and bad, a business flourishes based on the strength and authenticity of its culture. And the way a customer interacts with the brand is a major part of that.

Companies with strong, anchored service cultures will grow and prosper, while those with weak, frail customer cultures will wilt and eventually die.

Here's one unquestionable truth bomb we will explore further: stellar service trumps product, price, convenience, technology and theme every time. Always has; always will.

Out of everything I share during the course of the book, consider *that* mantra as the predominant melody for the entire anthem. Yes, I will provide specific examples and suggestions along the way— some perhaps are too lofty and grandiose for you, while others are no-brainers that you can implement tomorrow with immediate results—but never forget that delivering mind-searing, unforgettable customer experiences is the special sauce to differentiation.

Get that right and the results will practically be guaranteed.

GREATEST HIT

1 **Create legendary customer experiences to affect culture**—companies with strong, anchored service cultures will grow and prosper, while those with weak, frail customer cultures will wilt and eventually die.

I'm one of those
regular weird people.

JANIS JOPLIN

DIFFERENTIATION LEADS TO NIRVANA

ARE YOU flabbergasted when you experience truly great service? I know I am. Most consumers do not regularly receive fantastic customer service, so they are generally not used to it. It is clear, however, that great service fuels the fire of success. Sure, there's something to be said for being loyal to a local joint or even sticking to what we know based on consistency and familiarity, but most of us crave a different type of service experience. One that takes us aback, pleasantly surprises us and exceeds expectations ... the type of experience that's different than what everyone else is offering. We all want to feel special and be catered to as individuals.

Unfortunately, very few companies have capitalized on this "make me feel special" approach. The businesses that focus on this concept know that it's key to their sustainable success and work diligently to build it into their organizational culture.

Great customer experiences are not the result of a one-time program or annual initiative; they are generated through authentic customer-obsessed tendencies and are always a central part of the brand's day-to-day behaviors.

For example, Hard Rock is the physical manifestation of rock and roll for many fans of the brand. In a sense, it is as close to raw music and rock icons as the average person will ever get. Every time you walk into one of the branded venues, it's as though you've just entered a concert arena and have front row seats to see your favorite band. That's the experience Hard Rock tries to create for each and every guest.

The real connection, however, occurs with the staff. Hard Rockers are the bridge between the guests and the spirit of rock and roll, the cultural backbone of the company.

You might be shocked to discover that Hard Rock's service model includes irreverence and unpredictability—that's the tight rope the brand walks to deliver high-quality standards with an attitudinal flair. Great service pumped through an amplifier. Employees are taught to always be respectful, but also to help their guests take a walk on the wild side. That combination often creates memorable experiences. It's also a combination that few other brands would dare attempt, keeping them firmly mired in the world of mediocrity.

"To be Rock... I can't see us being vanilla ice cream. There's nothing wrong with vanilla, but people need a little chocolate in their lives... and I think that's what we provide. We get to be the chocolate," said Mike Kneidinger, the former VP of Company Cafes, Hard Rock International, and the retired president of Yard House restaurants. This former company executive used this analogy in training classes when he talked about the brand representing rock and roll and battling against mediocrity. In the land of ice cream, creating a unique service experience is about being the chocolate in a world full of vanilla.

Sometimes reinventing company culture through customer service is about being different. It is about finding the societal norm and then going against the grain, swimming upstream while everyone else takes the path of least resistance.

WORK EXPERIENCE IS NOT ENOUGH

We may think we need years of experience in every position, but we don't. Work experience is not enough. In fact, *repetition* of mediocre service practices only leads to *engrained* mediocre service practices. The ability to deliver unique guest experiences is far more valuable than an employee's tenure doing the same job year after year. People expect more. We need "different."

There is value in being different, both financially and strategically. The best employers "hire for attitude and train for skill," a notion that rings true today more than ever. Of course, we would also like experienced, competent, smart, hard-working employees, but these are often not the ones who will create memories for customers. Unique and unpredictable people truly leave lasting impressions on consumers.

IN A WORLD OF VANILLA ICE CREAM, BE THE CHOCOLATE.

———

SERVICE UNIQUENESS GETS REWARDED

Unique and unforgettable employee-to-customer interactions separate rock star brands from their competitors. They are internally celebrated by the company and externally recognized in the public domain.

Hard Rock International uses collectible service pins as a reward to team members who exceed specific guest satisfaction scores on a customer survey or mystery shopper's report. The company-pin culture at Hard Rock is unbelievable. So when, during a pre-shift team meeting, for example, an employee is recognized with a pin for great service, that desired behavior is more likely to be duplicated by their peers. As an added benefit, the best service-oriented Hard Rockers also get scheduled for their preferred shifts, allowing them to make more money or establish their own work-life balance.

Externally, the unique service provided is what guests like most about the Hard Rock brand. Customer surveys and consumer brand health studies validate this. Loyal fans certainly love the music-and-memorabilia environment, but the overall experience provided by the employees is what lures people back time and time again. Everyone wins with repeat business, which is a key component in the organization's sustainability.

Again, being different has its benefits.

This unique approach translates into a tremendous responsibility for the thousands of global team members who wear the Hard Rock logo, and one they collectively take very seriously. Frontline employees know that they cannot simply deliver on basic service standards. That's the bare minimum for staying in the game. It's what they do *additionally* that creates memorable experiences. If staff members were content with only delivering basic service, the organization would fall into the same forgettable malaise that so many others deliver. Mediocre. Middle of the road. Boring. Nothing special.

The notion that uncompromising service delivered by an authentic employee is the way to customers' hearts permeates the overall attitude of the Hard Rock brand. You too can channel this attitude to create your own service culture that rocks.

WALK THE LINE

Here are a just a few ways in which employees
can provide customer service that's different than
the norm:

- Rather than delivering a memorized script, greet
  customers authentically, using generational-speak
  appropriate for the specific customer.

- Interact with people while you ride together in a
  guest elevator—something that some businesses
  still see as taboo.

- Make genuine eye contact with shoppers standing
  in line to purchase something; give them the look,
  head nod or verbal confirmation of "I'll be right
  with you."

- Move at lightning speed in response to every
  customer's request, even if they are the only
  customer around.

- Heighten your awareness during customer
  interactions to identify and anticipate any needs the
  consumer may have, but also to listen intently to
  what they are saying.

- Look for connection opportunities with customers to make them feel special, by authentically complimenting their T-shirt logo, cool hair or stylish shoes.

Would any of these actions contradict your brand image? Are some of them too over-the-top for you? Do you wonder how your customers will react or worry about the types of interactions your staff might initiate? Only *you* can answer these questions, based on how open you are to change *and* how receptive you believe your company would be to walking the line of unpredictability. You may not implement all or even any of these ideas—but be aware that your risk-taking competitors may.

More and more, people today want uniqueness in their service experience. The baseline for service has been raised. Average is no longer good enough. Excellence is the new standard.

In fact, my mentality is to shoot for perfection, but settle for excellence.

Buc-ee's

Originally founded as a convenience store in Texas in 1982, Buc-ee's has grown to over fifty locations in multiple states and is now a coveted destination for road warriors and an experiential mecca for all.

Named after one of the co-founder's childhood names and his dog Buck, Buc-ee's is an experience like no other. Among its many accolades and boasts, Buc-ee's holds world records for the largest convenience store and the longest car wash. Additionally, after a nationwide contest, Cintas declared the brand's restrooms the cleanest in America. With spacious well-lit stalls that boast hand sanitizer inside, oversized sinks and mirrors, permanent restroom attendants and full-time security patrolling the entrances, it almost makes the roadside restrooms the main attraction. It certainly isn't the gas—even with fifty to a hundred pumps available at each location and prices usually 10 cents cheaper than any other gas around.

All Buc-ee's locations are open 24 hours a day, 365 days a year, serving fresh hot food made to order, including jerky, homemade fudge and all manner of snacks—both national brands and the more popular Buc-ee's brand. The company's signature Beaver Nuggets, which are large flavored corn puffs, have been

SHOOT FOR PERFECTION, BUT ONLY SETTLE FOR EXCELLENCE.

———

described as Kellogg's Corn Pops turned up to eleven and are the snack of choice for loyal fans. It's impossible to stop eating after a handful of Beaver Nuggets.

Since its home state is known for barbecue, it's no surprise that the counter in the center of the store is called the "Texas Round Up," which is populated with team members clad in denim aprons and yellow cowboy hats who regularly shout when there's fresh brisket on the chopping block. The team members on display are part of the overall experience. And, for the record, although the brisket and pulled pork are both worth snagging for an easy lunch, the sausage on a stick is the clear winner.

Once again, you would think Buc-ee's unique product and environment would be enough to guarantee success, but it is not. That is just the stage for the company's rock star employees to perform on. Buc-ee's employees truly seem genuine in their quest to provide friendly and fast Southern hospitality to customers—whether first-time visitors who are getting their minds blown or regulars who have gone out of their way to stop at the highway pitstop for a handcrafted breakfast burrito. The customer-centric approach is quickly pushing Buc-ee's to the top of the charts.

And experience-starved consumers are noticing.

Capital One

Capital One is now one of the major banks in the United States. While banks are traditionally stodgy, Capital One has amped up its unique offerings and service delivery to potential and existing customers.

The unique benefits of being a Capital One cardmember position the bank as a differentiator in the industry. The benefits include no fees on many transactions, no minimum account limits, the ability to lock the card yourself if it's missing and price protection and extended warranties on card purchases. These benefits alone would entice people to take a hard look at starting with or moving their banking to Capital One, but the company leadership knew that the "product" itself would not be enough. Hence the creation of Capital One Cafes, a combination coffee shop and bank branch all in one.

Rather than have traditional bank tellers, Capital One Cafes have "ambassadors" to answer your questions in a relaxed environment ... over coffee. The cafes have kiosks where you can open a no-fee checking or savings account in minutes or talk to a money coach about financial questions at a scheduled one-on-one coaching appointment. Each cafe typically offers free WiFi, plenty of power outlets, local snacks and Peet's Coffee (at a 50 percent discount for any of their handcrafted beverages). Several Capital One Cafes even have a community room that certain groups such as nonprofits, alumni, and students can book for free.

Capital One is clearly obsessed with making every touch point for the customer a positive one, whether online or in person. Although banking is a part of most people's lives, with its product offering, inviting environment and the connection established between ambassadors and cardmembers, the brand has set the stage for enjoyable experiences for their customers—not the words you would regularly associate with banking.

Whether you're the largest convenience store on the side of a highway or a major financial institution, being unique among your competitive set has its rewards. Your company does not have to be big or go big to stand out... but stand out you must.

What could you do to create differentiation?

That's what leads to customer nirvana.

GREATEST HITS

1 Hire for personality and culture fit over amount of experience—the ability to deliver unique customer experiences is far more valuable than an employee's tenure at the same job year after year.

2 Reward service uniqueness—unique and unforgettable employee-to-customer interactions separate rock star brands from their competitors.

3 Create competitor differentiation—your company does not have to be big or go big to stand out... but stand out you must.

I don't ever want to
do anything mediocre.

AMY WINEHOUSE

FOUR-
LETTER
WORDS

WHEN CANADIAN marketing guru, speaker and author Ron Tite appeared on *Thoughts That Rock*—the weekly leadership podcast I cohost with Brant Menswar—he started our conversation with a story.

He was at a brunch cafe on Queen West in Toronto when he noticed, at a nearby table, a family that was visibly frustrated over their waiter's lack of urgency, service indifference and overall disrespect for their time. Flustered, the family gathered their things to leave without eating, but then unintentionally encountered the waiter on their way out. The father loudly announced, "This is the worst service we have ever experienced. We're leaving!" Without missing a beat, and with complete apathy, the waiter simply said, "Dude, I'm in a band." As if that were acceptable or made it right.

When it comes to service, it's easy for some companies to succeed these days because so many others aren't even trying. The bar is set extremely low. Most companies wallow around in Pleasantville— where everything is "shades of gray" safe—offering completely forgettable service.

This may be because there are fewer role models to emulate these days. Few companies really ooze fantastic customer service. The truly standout service companies have seemingly all but disappeared. Sadly, we live in an era where great guest service is no longer the norm, but rather the exception. Companies talk about it and executives are aware of it, yet few address it—even those who are supposed to be running service-oriented companies.

THE PREDICTABLE QUAGMIRE

When a guest interaction is stuck in this mediocre quagmire, you can spot it; just listen to the verbal cues customers give when they're asked about their experience. Look for the predictable "four-letter words" that I believe will eventually put a company out of business (no, not *those* four-letter words). Ask a guest, "How is everything?" and if the experience is pretty forgettable, you'll hear one of the following four-letter words:

- Fine
- Good
- Okay

These words scream mediocrity. At the very least, the customers are not getting great service. The interaction doesn't have to be poor—just forgettable. A guest does not have to be venomous and blatantly upset with the service for it to make a negative difference in your company's success. In fact, being forgettable can be worse than being just plain bad. When service is *bad*, you often can salvage the experience and even blow away the customer's initial expectations with some savvy service recovery techniques.

If your company is forgettable, it leaves no lasting impression and little reason for customers to ever return. You are run-of-the-mill, average, typical and ordinary. This mediocre strategy leaves little hope for any brand's sustainability.

AVOIDING THE FORGETTABLE

To avoid four-letter words, your company may have to change some of its service practices. You might start by adjusting the way you ask people about their experience.

When you ask, "How is everything?" in a very casual and uninterested way, then you can expect a four-letter response that matches the tone of your question: "Fine." Consumers are so used to this question that they have developed automatic responses that connote as much emotion and care as the person who asked, "Everything okay?"

One way to avoid this type of response is to ask specifically about the food item, the hotel room or the theme park ride. That specificity will provide you with the type of realistic feedback you want, but also will most likely influence the customer to engage with you a bit more. Everybody wins here, as an authentic moment is created for the consumer.

Another way to minimize these four-letter-word responses is to alter the customer environment. If you create an environment that supports the mission of having a customer-obsessed service mentality, the end user will respond differently when asked how their experience is going. In brands that have hired and trained individuals to make solid eye contact, authentically smile at people, move as if they can't move fast enough for the guests and cater to customers' every need to their surprise and delight, it's doubtful that, when prompted, consumers will respond with a simple, unemotional "Good" or "Okay." It's more likely that you'll hear "It's awesome!" or "This place rocks!"

ACCEPTABLE MEDIOCRITY HURTS EVERYONE

Unfortunately, lukewarm service is so prevalent in our society that most people no longer even recognize it as such. It's simply the norm. In fact, customer service that doesn't verge on being poor is not only accepted; it's expected.

This revealing quote from Ken Blanchard's book *Raving Fans* says it all: "People expect bad goods and rude service. If the abuse isn't worse than they expected, they'll be back for more."

This mindset has created what I call "acceptable mediocrity." And we have all contributed to its creation. In many cases, apathy is the ultimate culprit. The employee or employees simply didn't care—or at least didn't appear to care. And apathy contributes to mediocrity being widely accepted.

I'm sure that at one time or another, you have experienced an apathetic interaction with a person or a company, only to shrug it off because you like the product, the price point or the convenient location. Other times, however, you let it go because you're used to tepid service. By allowing this totally forgettable interaction to go unaddressed, we endorse its continuation. This is acceptable mediocrity.

BRAVE PEOPLE VOTE WITH THEIR FEET

Every once in a while, the combination of mediocre service and an uncaring attitude creates enough of a bad experience that someone decides to act. The customer either points out the poor experience to a supervisor, leaves a negative online review, takes the time to call or write a letter to the corporate office or simply leaves, vowing never to return to the establishment because of the poor experience. The latter is the ultimate stance on one's principles, hitting the business where it hurts the most: its profit margin.

Brave people vote with their feet. Deciding to not shop, eat or stay somewhere based on a consistently uncaring or poor experience says a lot

DON'T ENDORSE ACCEPTABLE MEDIOCRITY BY ALLOWING IT TO EXIST.

——

about one's personal integrity. But most of the time, we don't stand on principle; we eventually crawl back to the establishment because of the product, the price or the convenience. Today, many consumers give these notions far greater value than the actual service provided. For them, great service is an artifact, rarely experienced and, even worse, hardly cared about by the business. This cyclical relationship *has* to come to an end.

We have to break the chain and reinvigorate companies with pure, uncut quality service.

This is a critical part of creating and maintaining a strong company culture. As part of your company's mission to enhance its overall culture, mediocre service must be avoided at all costs. Being forgettable is the fastest way to help your competition become the headlining act. Here are a few suggestions to specifically help you avoid mediocrity:

- Hire employees who naturally battle against the mundane because it's in their nature.

- Recommit and retrain every employee to become customer obsessed.

- Enhance your recognition and rewards for those employees who go above and beyond in providing customer service.

- Convene with your staff regularly and discuss how to differentiate your brand from others.

- Take risks in delivering a product or service with a fresh, unpredictable approach.

- Join networking associations to understand what your competitors are doing, then do something unique.

UNINTENTIONAL CONSEQUENCES

Sometimes, the customer's experience is affected negatively by a single moment. It may be unintentional, but nevertheless enough to derail the entire experience. There are literally hundreds of details we have to get right for customers to feel they've had a positive, even memorable, experience. Yet it only takes a single moment for it to go sideways. One misstep can ruin it all.

I can't tell you the number of times I have visited a restaurant where everything was perfect, from the time I parked my car to the moment I asked for the bill, only to find myself stuck in the last phase of the experience, emphatically scanning the room for my server, waiting interminably to pay the bill.

That single lack-of-awareness moment, even at the very end of the experience, negated all the perfect practices that came before it. Was it intentional? Absolutely not. But this part of the experience is fundamental to any restaurant's service model. A key tenet in the food and beverage world is to never let the guests wait to pay. What was looking to be a memorable and successful experience for me turned into a below average, forgettable one... and it happened at the drop of a hat. Just *that* quick to go from great to poor, because of a single person's behavior. The worst part is that most poor-service examples like these are absolutely avoidable. That is true for any industry.

Let me share a sobering example with you.

In May 2021, my father was diagnosed with colon cancer. After one session of chemotherapy and a week of trying to take care of him at home, my mother and I were forced to admit him into the hospital. Although this was an aggressive disease with many debilitating health symptoms, my dad was alert and in fairly good spirits throughout his hospital stay.

During the twenty-eight consecutive days he was in the oncology ward at a well-known health facility located in Central Florida, I spent almost every moment of every day by his side, tending to both his physical needs—especially when a nurse was not readily available—and his psychological state of mind. Those days were the toughest of my life. However, this hospital brand had thought of everything. The room's space, design and view were spectacular. The patient amenities, food quality and hospital cleanliness were fantastic. The lightning-quick WiFi and smart technology were all state of the art. Even so, the overall "product" did not come close to the rock star service we had experienced there. That is... until the final night of our stay.

Each night I had regularly stayed an hour or two beyond the official visiting hours to assist the nurses and patient technicians to change and clean my overweight father, who had become paralyzed during his hospital visit and required at least three people to perform this function without severe pain for him. Nightly leadership and staff regularly saw me during these moments and completely understood my presence. Many were thrilled to have my assistance. However, on the final, voluntary night of my father's hospital stay before moving to end-of-life hospice, an uncaring and power-driven charge nurse—let's call her Liz—instructed me to immediately leave (since visiting hours had ended two hours ago). During our brief exchange, I tried to explain how I had been there with the team caring for my father every night of his stay, that he was transferring in the morning, and all the physical reasons why it was appropriate for me to be there. (I will spare you the heartbreaking and messy details.) I even mentioned that my family had such a positive experience over the last twenty-seven days that I'd bought premium Crumbl Cookies for the entire floor earlier that day, as a small thank-you for their tireless hospitality.

All that seemed to fall on the deaf ears of unempathetic Charge Nurse Liz. She insisted I leave immediately or she would have security escort me out of the hospital; that they did not need my help and could handle everything on their own. After unsuccessfully pleading with Liz a final time, I left and logged a formal complaint on the hospital's website, which never garnered a response.

The following morning, after he was transported to a hospice facility, my father passed away. I never had an opportunity to talk with him again, especially about this final experience, but Liz's interaction with him was the last forever-seared memory we have of this hospital brand. That was all it took: one negative moment from an uncaring employee to completely ruin a month-long, mostly positive experience.

I can clearly see why this health care brand, one of the largest in the country, receives some of the highest awards and accolades possible; they exceed in almost every area. But for me, Liz is the brand. That is how I now think of this health care company.

And, unfortunately, with a different set of four-letter words.

BANISHED FOREVER

In any situation, if the unfavorable service is unintentional and the overall product, price and experience is still positive, it's much easier to forgive a mistake once and simply hope the behavior isn't the norm. In scenarios like that, I would most likely give the business another shot. However, if the service is flat-out poor, consistently lackadaisical or, even worse, completely horrific because of a single moment created by an employee, then that business becomes one of the places forever etched onto my "no-go" list, banished for all time, with zero hope of a future visit.

My father's end-of-life story may be a bit extreme in a chapter focused on how mediocre service ultimately affects the long-term health of the brand, but all bad service experiences are born from the same place: human behavior. And those unfavorable experiences are completely avoidable.

GREATEST HITS

1 **Battle against the mundane**—it's so easy for companies to succeed these days because so many others aren't even trying. Those that aspire to change their service culture need only spend a little energy and focus on their staff-to-customer interactions to become memorable and separate themselves from the rest.

2 **Blast apart "acceptable mediocrity"**—if you allow totally forgettable, mediocre interactions to occur with customers (which lead to four-letter words—"good," "fine," "okay"), you endorse its continuation.

3 **Hire people who deliver spectacular service**—unfavorable customer service experiences from employees are born out of learned human behavior... and are completely avoidable.

I still have an insane
drive to create and
express myself,
and it'll never stop
because I don't know
how to stop it.

GRAHAM NASH

CUSTOMER OBSESSION PRODUCES SUSTAINABILITY

THE ROLLING STONES, arguably one of the greatest rock and roll bands of all time, were the highest-grossing concert act every time they went on the road—especially in their later years. It wouldn't matter if the band produced or sold a new record ever again, they would still sell out each and every show, even while commanding a premium price. And people would pay it—just to watch Mick Jagger and Keith Richards do their thing on stage. Fans lucky enough to get tickets to a Stones show were willing to pay the price *for* the show, *because of* the show. And they did this time and time again. It did not matter how many times these "lifers" saw The Rolling Stones; if the band was in town, its dedicated and determined followers would find a way to see it.

People repeat what they like.

The same is true in every business that provides a service. If a company provides service that exceeds the consumer's expectations, a return visit is almost guaranteed. So it is no coincidence that many of the great service stories you hear reference the same companies: brands that continue to produce consistent and healthy results.

SERVICE MISSION #1: BECOME OBSESSED

As you compare companies within a competitive set, the value of service becomes even more apparent. There are many examples of companies with products nearly indistinguishable from their competitors, yet one flourishes while the other flounders. In these cases, history will often prove that the single differentiator between success and failure was the service each company provided to consumers—not the physical product being sold. The winners were the ones obsessed with the overall customer experience that made service delivery a top priority. The losers missed the point completely. Customer obsession produces sustainability.

Service delivery is just as important to the long-term success of the business as the product itself.

Best Buy

U.S. technology retail giants Best Buy and Circuit City are prime examples. Virtually identical in their inceptions and basic product offerings, these competitors couldn't have been further apart in their approach to the market. Where Circuit City relied solely on the products it sold, Best Buy prided itself on fostering a customer-obsessed mentality. That basic differentiation rendered Circuit City obsolete, forcing it to close its doors forever in 2009. It was quickly apparent that while these stores swam in the same pond, they were oceans apart in consumer service.

Although Best Buy experiences organizational issues from time to time, the company took a preferably different path than Circuit City—and the public is better off because of it. Brand advocates of Best Buy can only hope that the company does not fall into the same trap as its competitors and lose sight of the thing that made it great in the first place: a customer-centric service philosophy.

SERVICE CULTURE VETERANS

In this chapter, you will find numerous examples of world-class, service-oriented companies, each of which I consider "monsters of rock." They are The Rolling Stones of the service industry. Some of them will not be the "usual suspects" you think of or have even heard of. Perhaps, within this collection of a few service culture faves, you will find the spark you need to change your company's internal service culture.

Here are some of the well-known brands that have always stood out to me.

Nordstrom

Department store giant Nordstrom is one of those companies with a decades-long run of providing great experiences directly to its consumers. Surely by now you've heard the infamous story of how a customer returned an unsatisfactory set of tires and received a refund from the store. This story defined Nordstrom's service culture—largely because of the fact that Nordstrom doesn't sell tires. The in-the-moment decision by a single employee to accommodate a person who was not even a Nordstrom customer has become the story-heard-round-the-world and the stuff of legends.

Are you (or your sales staff) bold enough to take back an item without a receipt or proof of purchase... or even an item not sold by your company? Because customer-focused cultures like Nordstrom's do this without fear. And those organizations are creating new fans every day.

Disney

The Walt Disney World organization is also a master at service. When founder Walt Disney sought to create the Magic Kingdom, he purposefully focused on every detail of the guest's theme park visit so he could better control the overall experience. A swarm of human street sweepers are let loose in the park daily to keep immaculate order. Hedges are clipped and grass is mowed at night to keep up the illusion of perfection in the guests' eyes. Buildings, rides and natural landscape are all designed to keep you from catching even a remote "behind the curtain" view of the park's inner machinery. Yes, everything is purposefully themed— but all of that only sets the stage for the real magic: guest interactions with "cast members."

In the initial on-boarding program, "Traditions," all Disney cast members are taught fundamental service principles that include the art of creating "magical memories." In a nutshell, Disney teaches each of its 200,000 employees that they are empowered to take a moment during their scheduled shifts to create an experience so memorable that the guests involved will not forget the interaction for the rest of their lives. These unforgettable moments are called "magical memories." And these moments transcend theme parks. The perfectly hired and highly trained cast members at an offsite, standalone Disney retail store or serving aboard Disney Cruise Lines are providing the same "magical memories" designed to change people's lives.

This simple concept has aligned an entire global workforce with Disney's signature service culture.

Starbucks

Starbucks is so engrained into our daily lives, and it is a service beacon in many ways. I mean, the company is solely responsible for making coffee cool. But it's not just about the coffee, is it? Loyal fans of the company love just about everything the brand does: its quality product, the trendy artwork on the walls, a mix of overstuffed and ergonomic furniture, a leading-edge approach to fair trade practices, socially conscious initiatives and more. But it's the personalized service provided by quick and knowledgeable baristas that makes Starbucks a daily routine for millions. You get in, out and caffeinated quickly and efficiently with the help of a pleasant and professional employee who probably looks and behaves just a little bit differently than coffee shop employees looked and behaved before Starbucks came along.

While Starbucks' service practices may not be as top-of-mind as they used to be for many, they were one of the first to truly make me feel special. Whether it's the blazing speed at which my complicated coffee order is made, the barista writing my name on the cup—no one had done that before—or the way they commit my customized drink to memory, their obsession created loyalty.

I actually refer to the company as "Fivebucks," because that's what I'm willing to spend for every cup of the Starbucks experience—five dollars. I could go elsewhere, pay less and wait in a shorter line for a premium cup of coffee, but Starbucks has earned my

business with its service delivery. This experience
is worth my five bucks, two times a day, five days
a week. Do the math. I am willing to spend thousands
of dollars a year at Starbucks when I could just drink
the free coffee at work or spend 10 percent of that
cost by brewing it at home.

PRODUCT IS NEVER ENOUGH

While there is no debate about the product quality
of the legendary companies I have mentioned here,
product alone is not enough. Being customer obsessed
and making service delivery a top priority is just
as important to the long-term success of the business.
In fact, the *delivery* of an experience is now more
critical to overall customer perception than anything
else. The rest of the experience is purely "bricks and
mortar" and will never be enough to separate the
mediocre companies from the great ones.

Don't get me wrong, product quality is still
massively important, but in today's world of
experiential thrill-seekers and value hawks, great
product is now a given. It's the price of admission.

The consumer needs more.

GREAT PRODUCT IS JUST THE PRICE OF ADMISSION.

———

Chick-fil-A

One of the great business cultures that enjoys an almost cult-like following is Chick-fil-A, an American quick-service chicken restaurant. The company's product is fantastic, often touted as the best chicken sandwich in the food industry. But as great as the product is, it's not the reason I assign the company rock icon status. This cultural fave of mine tops the charts because of its "irreverence" and "unpredictability." These might seem like odd word choices for describing Chick-fil-A, but I believe this brand marches to the beat of a different drum than its competitors.

It is widely known by the general public that this privately held company has a faith-based heritage, one that sparked some controversy when the brand's founder made some personal religious comments in a published interview. These comments turned off quite a few members of the public, even leading to a boycott of the restaurants. But they also caused even *more* fans to rally around the company, solidifying its unique culture in *their* eyes. And it has paid off, big time. In 2010, well before the controversy,

Chick-fil-A surpassed McDonald's to claim the number-one spot in single store sales, and it now generates an average of $4.9 million in annual revenue per location, versus the hamburger chain's $2.4 million. And Chick-fil-A is doing it without operating twenty-four hours a day, or outside North America... and with fewer operating days. Because of the company's faith and family philosophy, its restaurants are closed on Sundays.

This amazing story continues to be written.

Chick-fil-A realizes that product—as good as it is—is not enough. It is only part of the equation that contributes to the company's years of growth, financial success and rightful place as one of the world's great service culture warriors. The key ingredient in this recipe for success is the employee.

As many fans of the restaurant chain will attest, Chick-fil-A is "religious" about the people it brings on board to represent the company. I mean that literally. Whether you're a fan of the brand or not, you can't dispute that it hires "right fit" employees. In fact, company management goes to great lengths to ensure it. In addition to having a customer-obsessed philosophy, each associate's value system matches up with that of the organization. As closely aligned as the harmonies on a Beatles tune, there is no conflict between personal interest and the brand's ultimate mission. So the attention to detail, sense of urgency and genuine care demonstrated by employees doesn't just come across as authentic—it *is* authentic. When an employee responds to every request with "It's my pleasure" I actually believe that it's their pleasure to be positive and helpful.

When I go to Chick-fil-A, I usually go through the drive-thru because it's quick. I cannot say that about any other fast food joint, but even if the line of cars circles the building twice, I have no problem jumping into the fray; I know it will still only be a few minutes to get my order and carry on. The associates' sense of urgency is valuable to me. But just as comforting is their attention to detail. To this day, I have never experienced a mistake in my drive-thru order at Chick-fil-A. Never. Again, I cannot say the same about any other quick-service business.

Just recently, I stopped by Chick-fil-A for lunch and went inside to order. As I stood at the order counter, I had a wide stance and my hands on my hips in curiosity while I contemplated the menu board.

When I finally made eye contact with Jose, the quick-witted employee at the register, he instinctively said, "Well, hey there, Peter Pan!" alluding to the way I was standing—exactly as the character stands in the book and movie and on stage. We both immediately busted out laughing.

That was *it*. That was the moment that this employee turned me into a lifelong, raving fan.

Here was an attentive personality who understood the value of being on the hunt for a moment of opportunity... and then pouncing on it. Without being offensive or condescending, he took a risk to provide some unpredictability. Instead of letting that "low-hanging fruit" moment pass, like most businesses would probably prefer, Jose took advantage of that window to create something memorable for me. And it worked. I have never remembered the name of an employee at a fast food restaurant before, but I won't ever forget Jose's. In that singular moment, this individual rocked my world and solidified my loyalty.

Well done, Chick-fil-A. Well done.

LESSONS FROM THE GIANTS

We can learn a lot from legends. I am going to share personal stories from some lesser-known customer-obsessed businesses, but first let's embrace the best practices from some of the iconic industry dominators I just discussed. They each provide a compelling blueprint for differentiation. Here are just a few lessons to take away:

- Take great care when thinking through what you want your company's service culture to be... before it gets too big to effectively maintain.

- Surround yourself with competent decision-makers who act in the best interest of the customer and the brand, especially when leadership is not around.

- Empower your employees to create "magical memories" with their customers.

- Never stop developing the service culture, regardless of the company's size.

It is not a single story but a definitive service culture, rich in a heritage of customer obsession, that defines service-veteran organizations like Nordstrom, Disney, Starbucks and Chick-fil-A.

And for that, I am a fan of each.

GREATEST HITS

1 Turn one-time customers into devoted, loyal fans—if a company provides service that exceeds the consumer's expectations, a return visit is practically guaranteed.

2 Be obsessive about service to produce sustainability—making service delivery a top priority of an experience is now more critical to overall customer perception than anything else. The rest of the experience will never be enough to separate the mediocre companies from the great ones.

3 Study the blueprints of giants—embrace the lessons and best practices from big, iconic industry dominators to provide direction for differentiation and sustainability.

You can't knock on opportunity's door and not be ready.

BRUNO MARS

5

LEGENDARY EXPERIENCES COME IN EVERY SIZE

AWORLD-CLASS service culture does not happen by accident. It has to be developed constantly and fostered by leaders who understand how critical it is to the company's reputation and ultimate success. The overall customer experience—or CX—is everything to them. And it should be for you.

Regional brands like Publix supermarkets and Sheetz convenience stores are starting to get more national recognition because of this very approach. As great as their products and environments are, the stellar and consistent service delivered to their customers is the true differentiator.

As much as Starbucks' founder and CEO Howard Schultz focused on the product and the atmosphere, he knew that the way in which coffee was delivered mattered just as much. As the brand began to scale beyond a single store in Seattle, it required a heightened focus on the customer experience as one of the company's key value offerings.

This is something to consider if you are a small business on the cusp of expanding your brand. It is certainly not easy to come out of the gate with a phenomenal service culture as a budding business or single-location start-up, but it is definitely easier than being a massive organization trying to maintain or revolutionize a great one. When you are a small company, you have better control over all the nuances that go into delivering the customer experience. But once you cross the threshold of having multiple, geographically widespread locations and must rely on other company leaders to make local decisions about talent, systems and processes, the task of flawlessly executing memorable experiences becomes much more difficult.

SINGLE-LOCATION ICONS

Some businesses have focused on delivering a differentiated service experience so much that it transcends a single location. Not physically, but reputationally. Word on the street of the rock star service provided starts to permeate the industry, market and even country, ultimately becoming a regular name on top of brand health studies and cultural case studies.

Check out a few of my favorites, from which every service-oriented business could learn a thing or two.

Pike Place Fish Market

No company better exemplifies the idea of creating memorable experiences than the world-famous Pike Place Fish Market in Seattle, Washington. Most American business professionals are by now well-aware of the famed "fish throwers," whose unique delivery system started organically as a fun way for the fishmonger employees to sell fish.

Imagine working long, grueling shifts in a stinky environment, performing the same mundane tasks of stocking, selling and packing fish day after day. Not the usual place one would expect memorable service, but the employees did indeed create such an environment. It started with an attitude the brand calls its FISH! Philosophy. Employees were empowered to go beyond just filling orders and instead create an unforgettable experience for customers—not to mention an unparalleled work environment for each other, now envied by companies around the world.

The FISHmongers started by showcasing products for passersby with attentive service and witty banter, but then they took it to the next level by passionately and loudly announcing a customer's order before tossing the fish to another employee from across the market display. This unique experience was then perpetuated by being captured and shared with the business world through popular and inspiring educational FISH! videos, workbooks and seminars.

News of this unique culture at a local fish market quickly spread by word of mouth. Businesses everywhere began to see the immediate, applicable value of delivering memorable service in their own organizations, regardless of the industry or business type. The appeal was simple: if fishmongers could create a culture that rocks, then we can certainly figure out a way to create better experiences for *our* consumers.

This unexpected showmanship performed by a unique cast of characters is now legendary. In fact, Pike Place Fish Market is the number-one tourist destination in Seattle. Think about that: a single-location fish market as the ultimate attraction. Sounds unbelievable, but it's true.

These employees made the art of selling fish cool and relevant to the average customer. The overall experience is the reason the fishmonger is so popular— not the product itself.

Zappos

Zappos.com is another single-location icon that secured its place in the history of legendary service experiences because of the visionary approach to business and sheer will of the late founder and CEO Tony Hsieh.

Practically a household name now, Zappos is the Las Vegas–based online shoe retailer that started in 1999 selling other brands' shoes through the internet but made happiness the core of the company's culture and day-to-day mission. Hsieh knew that a great company culture leads to employee happiness, which would then drive higher engagement and profitability, and lower turnover. But it's the laser-like focus on delivering a "WOW!" experience to every customer that makes the company so unique. Expressly listed in its purpose and core values, Zappos' customer-centric culture can be summed up by the only important directive employees have: that the customer is happy—no matter what.

Blasting it out there for the world to see, Zappos' website proudly states, "We are not an average company, our service is not average, and we don't want our people to be average. We expect every employee to deliver WOW." And they do. Any time I facilitate a discussion on culture with an audience, specifically when I am soliciting what the most admired service-oriented brands are, Zappos always makes the list.

So, just how are the employees maniacally obsessed with making their customers happy? The best list I have seen to date that captures this service approach was in an article written by Roxanne Warren and posted on the Zappos website, which highlights these ten fundamentals:

1. It's easy to connect with customer service because it's impossible not to find the phone number: it's everywhere on the website and company vehicles.

2. A customer service rep will stay on the phone for as long as it takes to solve a problem. Their current record is almost eleven hours!

3. The phone reps truly love talking with customers and make it their mission to provide the best solutions. A customer receiving a mailed greeting card from their new friend at Zappos is not unusual.

4. Customers don't have to navigate multiple steps or automated recordings, since a real person answers every call in less than a minute.

5   Phone reps don't have scripts. Instead, they have real conversations about everything from order exchanges to kids, pets and sports.

6   The call center operates 24/7 to accommodate any schedule.

7   Phone reps are empowered with management-level decision-making authority to provide unique and appropriate solutions.

8   Customers have an entire year to return an item. Unheard of.

9   Shipping and returns are free and fast.

10 Phone reps never upsell to try to get customers to buy more than they planned.

You have to remember that this is an online shoe company that sells other companies' shoes. Not a restaurant, hotel or theme park, but an internet-based shoe company. And yet the mind-searing experiences that every customer has when they interact with Zapponians help perpetuate the company's customer-obsessed reputation.

Zappos rocks!

Yellow Dog Eats

Twenty minutes from my home, in the Central Florida township of Gotha, lives one of the greatest restaurant "finds" around. Overshadowed by the unlimited amount of casual dining available in the greater Orlando area, Yellow Dog Eats was once only known to the locals. But as its reputation began to spread, even tourists discovered the small restaurant's website and eventually flocked to the location to experience the legendary service and fantastic food.

In a restaurant named after his beloved yellow Labrador retriever, throwback chef and entrepreneur Fish Morgan has carved out one of the trendiest places in the area. While the restaurant hangs its hat on serving mouth-watering classic sandwiches, soups and desserts with an eclectic twist, *that* is only a small fraction of the experience. The two-story house-turned-cafe is adorned with a potpourri of items: photos of yellow Labs, a handful of signed black-and-white celebrity photos, and jars of homemade jams, jellies, condiments and sauces. Most would consider this a pretty odd array of knick-knacks, but that's just part of the overall charm.

Yellow Dog Eats is located across the street from a church in the heart of a conservative community, and for many years zoning restrictions meant that Fish could only sell wine by the bottle. This would be a monumental handicap for many restaurants, as alcohol sales provide the largest profit potential—sometimes as much as 50 to 75 percent of the business's earnings. This challenge did not seem to faze Fish. In fact, it gave him an excuse to create an experiential window craved by the locals: free wine tastings in the evening to generate buzz and product demand. Still, this is but a backdrop to the overall experience. Without a doubt, the real secret ingredient to the business's success is Chef Fish Morgan.

After visiting the establishment dozens of times on my own, I began singing its praises and bringing friends to eat—all because of Fish. There was never a time when I brought a friend to Yellow Dog Eats that Fish did not come out of the kitchen or from behind the register to shake the new customer's hand, give him a huge embrace or even kiss her on the cheek. Not a common practice with complete strangers, but Fish pulls it off with a warm and welcoming disposition.

Chef Morgan certainly has an insatiable desire to talk. And he makes the most honest, off-the-cuff comments—usually the first thing that comes to his mind. At first contact, you would think his

MAKE PEOPLE FEEL SPECIAL AND THE CULTURE WILL THRIVE.

———

communication filter was removed at birth, but Fish's personality and approach is all by design. He gets it. He knows exactly what it takes to stand out in the consumer's mind, and his authenticity and attention to service is unparalleled in the area. He may talk about his ongoing battle with the city commission over serving wine by the glass or he may slide into describing the time and preparation it took to make his unique pulled pork, but every conversation with Fish is a breath of fresh air compared to your usual meal-time conversation with a restaurant manager. Along with fantastic food, the service culture this restaurant creates is the reason I continue to go back to Yellow Dog Eats and bring others with me.

You don't have to have an eclectic business or be the company's owner to create the same type of environment. You and the people you surround yourself with just need to be as passionate and committed to service as Fish is to rocking people's worlds. Approach every single customer as if they are a VIP or your best friend. Treat people like they're special, and their positive experience is practically guaranteed. Make people feel special and the culture will thrive.

BBB of Amarillo, Texas

Several years ago, I was hired to speak for the Better Business Bureau in Amarillo, Texas, at its annual Torch Awards for Ethics, which is an event to recognize exceptional organizations for their dedication to integrity and ethical business practices. It is the most prestigious honor the BBB can present to a company. Leaders from every type of business and industry in that market attend this awards dinner. To be the keynote speaker at this event was a great honor for me, and I was thrilled to be a part of it.

As I always do, I traveled to Amarillo from Orlando the day before to ensure that I would not miss the session, especially with the state of travel these days: chaotic and unreliable. In this case, since the event was an evening program, I had the rare luxury of being in the city for a full day before the event. What I anticipated to be a leisurely stroll through downtown shops and restaurants turned out to be one of the most memorable of my life.

Completely unbeknownst to me, the Better Business Bureau had marketed the event citywide, using my name and photo, which appeared on posters in business storefront windows and on restaurant table tents everywhere. Even wilder, they used the same

NOTHING IS MORE IMPORTANT THAN ROCKIN' THE CUSTOMER'S FACE OFF.

---

bold marketing in several highway billboards entering the city. My name and photo were everywhere! My mind was blown. I felt like a big-time celebrity.

As I meandered around the streets of this charming Texas town, business owners and a few Amarilloans recognized me—some even asking for a photo with me. I never did ask the event planner, Janna Kiehl, if they did this every year, for every keynote speaker, but it really didn't matter. The fact that they did it for *me* was special enough. This entire community made me feel incredible. The Amarillo BBB rocked my face off.

You certainly don't have to go this over-the-top, but what could you do to make your customers feel like rock stars?

There is a reason we continue to talk about service-oriented giants like Costco, Southwest and Ritz-Carlton, but we can also learn a lot from single-location icons like Pike Place, Zappos and Yellow Dog Eats: they create memories. Great sustainable brands—regardless of size—create unforgettable experiences.

Out of everything you do, there is nothing more important than rockin' the customer's face off (figuratively speaking, of course).

And the results will show.

GREATEST HITS

1 Act big, go big—by delivering mind-searing, differentiated service experiences for customers, a company can develop a shareable reputation that transcends a single location.

2 Commit to rockin' people's worlds—make people feel special, as if they were a VIP or your best friend, and the culture will thrive.

3 Aspire to be one of the great service cultures—if single-location brands like a fish market and an online shoe retailer can do it, any company can do it. All it takes is some collective willpower.

I want to be singing to everybody, and I want everybody to think that I'm singing to them.

JOAN JETT

LESSONS FROM "THE ROCK"

EMPLOYEES YEARN to be part of a great story. If people can connect to something important to them—or even something bigger than themselves—then asking them to deliver world-class service or create a premium product will be a much easier task. They will do it out of commitment to the brand, versus compliance with a boss. People will do things on behalf of the company not because they *have* to, but because they *want* to. They see the bigger picture and are emotionally involved. Compelling stories motivate people to provide amazing service to consumers. That's the power of great brands.

If your employees identify with your company's story and wholeheartedly believe in it, they will work hard to be positive and meaningful representatives of it.

ONE BRAND'S STORY

Hard Rock International is just such a brand. I believe Hard Rock's iconic heritage is one of the greatest stories in the history of stories, and it constantly inspires employees to work hard representing that story. The company's remarkable success—its ability to stand out among its competitive set—is legendary. And it is predominantly because of the organization's dedication to world-class service.

Since I spent twenty-one years with the company— a big portion of that time heading up training and development practices and perpetuating its culture— allow me to use the iconic music-oriented brand as a case study, specifically when it comes to customer service.

People familiar with Hard Rock will usually acknowledge that its service approach is worthy of high praise. Sure, the irreverent rock and roll environment is a great backdrop, but the heart of the brand is its guest service delivery, a performance indicator that regularly earns high marks on customer surveys. It's one of the things that people like the most about the company, and that's not by coincidence. The brand prides itself on being revolutionary when it comes to offering service that rocks. Its management and staff view every consumer's visit to its hotels, casinos and restaurants as an opportunity to change that person's expectations about exactly what top-notch service should look and feel like. Simply put, Hard Rock strives to become the measuring stick for all other companies.

Just as I share some of Hard Rock's fascinating lore and solid business practices here, the company does the same for the thousands of new hires drawn to this legendary brand. Facilitated New Hire Orientations, delivered around the world, are designed to inspire, motivate and even emotionally hook a person to the brand, with the understanding that these "rockers" will then deliver a spectacular and memorable service experience to their guests.

THE FOUNDERS

Hard Rock Cafe founders Isaac Tigrett and Peter Morton originally set out to create a Tennessee truck-stop diner in the United Kingdom. Their goal was to introduce the British to American comfort food like hamburgers, milkshakes, BBQ ribs and apple pie, but they also hoped to open a restaurant where everyone would be welcomed and treated the same, regardless of social status. They went to great lengths to ensure the delivery of premium quality products, the likes of which the English had never seen, and to develop a business model that would change the world: great American fare, flavored with a heavy dose of rock and roll, yet operating with a social conscience.

Still, it wouldn't be enough.

Even during Hard Rock's inception, Tigrett and Morton knew that unique service delivery would be the sustainable X factor in their business—the thing that would differentiate their product from all the others. So, their focus was on delivering unparalleled customer service and cutting-edge, but authentic, experiences.

RECREATE "MOM"

Tigrett and Morton's desire to create a place where everyone would be welcomed equally but serviced individually could only be fulfilled by the employees they hoped to hire. So, although the founders put tremendous thought, care and attention into every physical guest touch point in the restaurant, their greatest achievement was in hiring the right staff to deliver these unforgettable experiences. You might think they would have gone after a youthful employee base, but instead they only hired women that were at least thirty years old as their original servers.

Their approach sparks an interesting question: What was it about a thirty-year-old woman in the 1970s that, in the founders' eyes, made her uniquely capable of delivering experiences that would resonate with customers? For starters, she was the type of waitress you would *actually* find in a roadside diner or truck stop in the American South, which was the themed business model of the first Hard Rock Cafe. But their rationale transcended even *that* notion.

Their idea was simple: let's recreate "Mom."

It certainly didn't hurt that a more experienced service employee came with none of the perceived baggage of a nineteen-year-old, but that was just a small part of their reasoning when they selected the original staff.

Most of the London Hard Rock Cafe's original servers were plucked from local hotel restaurants and private clubs, but their technical expertise was also not the sole driving force behind the founders' decision. No doubt it helped in areas like attention to detail, sense of urgency and an impeccable work ethic, but

Tigrett and Morton determined right away that dining customers wanted to be treated as special, as if they were having dinner at their mother's house, where they would be constantly coddled. The personalized, organic and unpredictable experiences delivered by "Mom," the founders believed, would create unforgettable memories for their customers. This approach was quite forward-thinking at the time, but it wound up being the linchpin of the brand's long-term success.

WHAT WOULD MOM DO?

So, what does the type of server Hard Rock chose to hire more than fifty years ago have to do with a company's inner culture today?

Remember, this type of careful employee selection was revolutionary in the hospitality industry at the time. Nobody was doing it. And therein lies the point: Hard Rock managed to find a unique way to transform the way it offered its product, and that became the defining element of the brand's success.

When you consider shifting your company's culture through the way it presents products and services, you should be looking for a defining element—something unique compared to your direct competitors. In other words, you have to find your own way to recreate "Mom." Clearly, I don't mean that you should channel your inner mother. But to be a culture catalyst, you have to identify the best route for providing your service—and then figure out how to implement it in the inner workings of your organization.

Here are a few "What Would Mom Do?" suggestions for you to consider:

- Allow employees to be unique, different from everyone else. (Mom loved you exactly the way you were.)

- Make customers feel special, like they are guests in your home (the way Mom made you feel every time you walked into her house).

- Authentically connect with others, not as a technique but with genuine interest (just as Mom listened and paid attention to your every word).

Mom was right about a lot of things, and we could all learn a thing or two about making others feel special from her. In the next few pages, we'll review these basic motherly tenets as we go deeper into enhancing your company's execution of a product or service.

KISS MY GRITS

The most experienced talent is not always the right fit for your service approach. This may seem to fly in the face of the original approach to Hard Rock Cafe staffing, since Tigrett and Morton initially hired only mature women, but their approach was deliberate. Their reasoning had little to do with potential employees' previous experience or tenure in the industry. They were looking for a specific service mindset that would, they believed, create memorable experiences for guests.

And that required hiring unique employees.

To envision the prototypical employee that perhaps Morton and Tigrett sought, you'd have to be a fan of American television shows in the 1970s. Characters like Lucille Ball and, later, Carol Burnett infiltrated the airwaves and may have influenced the Hard Rock founders' idea of the perfect service conduit, but in my mind, no one fits the image of the quintessential Tennessee truck-stop diner waitress better than the irreverent character of Flo, of Mel's Diner, on the hit television show *Alice*. I'm sure those of you who are old enough can hear the immortal words "Kiss my grits!" ringing in your ears right now. Flo was known for chewing gum, complaining about the workload

THE MOST EXPERIENCED TALENT ISN'T ALWAYS THE RIGHT FIT.

———

and even slinging a few insults at the guests who pushed her buttons, but she also had her regulars who kept coming back for more—because she created experiences. She was one of a kind. She was real. She was memorable. She was unapologetically authentic.

The original Hard Rock Cafe servers were just like that. They were a bit irreverent and almost always unpredictable, but guests loved every moment of the experience because it was different. It was the spirit of rock and roll come to life. That edginess may not be as readily acceptable in today's society, your company or every market, but consumers still crave different. In a twenty-first-century Hard Rock environment, rock star employees know how to walk the line between being edgy and being disrespectful. Some questions for you to consider:

- What is your prototypical employee profile?
- Is there even an ideal employee for your brand?

When making your own hiring decisions, you have to first consider the type of mold you are trying to fill. It could be someone like Flo, or it could be very different: perhaps someone who is young, trendy and extremely attentive and polite. Every business has particular needs that should be evaluated before the hiring process even begins. But if you don't know the shapes of the holes, how can you find the pegs that will fit?

Another unquestionable truth I have come to embrace over the years: unique people create unique experiences. Of that, I am certain.

FROM WAITRESS TO MBE

To fill Hard Rock's employee ranks, it seemed as though "day one" servers, with mid-century diner names like Eve, Betty and Delia, were pulled right out of a classic black-and-white movie script—they looked and acted exactly as you'd imagine they would. Unlike the made-up television character Flo, these thirty-year-old spitfires were the real deal. They were one of a kind and memorable to anyone who shared a moment with them.

More than anyone else, original server Rita Gilligan became the company's quintessential rock star. It was an unintended role that she fell into, but one she gladly accepted.

Rita confided to me on a number of occasions that she didn't consider herself the best technical server around, but that her infectious personality and natural gift to talk saved her every day—and made her a lot of money at the time. Rita eventually owned several

UNIQUE PEOPLE CREATE UNIQUE EXPERIENCES.

—

homes—one for each of her kids—based on years of gratuities that fans showered her with because of the experiences she provided. I would say she made a pretty comfortable living out of her attitude.

Turning thirty just six days before the opening of the original Hard Rock Cafe, Rita barely met the company's hiring requirements when she was interviewed by Peter Morton. However, she ultimately became the face of the brand. And then the amazing happened. In 1998, because of her well-known service approach and years of dedication to tourism in the United Kingdom, Rita Gilligan was awarded the MBE (Member of the British Empire), the highest civilian award you can receive from the Royal Court.

Can you believe it? Rita started her career as a server more than twenty-five years before receiving this award, yet her uniqueness became legendary. So much so that an entire country recognized her outstanding performance in the service industry.

When she retired, Rita continued to act as the organization's "cultural attaché," spending the majority of her time spreading the heritage of Hard Rock. She told the early company stories as only she could, tracing Hard Rock's progress from the craziness of a fledgling cafe to the global entertainment brand it is today.

In fact, for many years the London Hard Rock Cafe displayed table tents informing guests that Rita would visit the restaurant on the first Thursday of every month, completely decked out in her perfect white diner dress, paper hat and collectible guitar pins. And she did—every week. She methodically made her way to every guest in the cafe to share stories, take pictures and sign autographs. Unless there was a major holiday in the U.K., "Rita Day" was one of the cafe's busiest days every month; customers flocked to get some one-on-one time with her.

I share Rita's story so that you understand how one rock star in the business can make a major impact. People were attracted to Rita because she offered them something they couldn't get anywhere else: an unbelievable cultural and service experience.

Consumers are categorically enthusiastic about differentiated experiences. When a company can combine quality product with fantastic service, the stars align and customers will be blown away. This is not unique to Hard Rock. For an organization that sells a product or delivers a service as its business model, this differentiation must be part of the brand culture. This is critical to its long-term future.

GREATEST HITS

1 **Share the brand's story with style**—
employees yearn to be part of a great story.
When they see the big picture and become
emotionally involved, they will willingly
deliver rock star customer service on behalf
of the company.

2 **Recreate "Mom"**—adopt the basic tenet that
the personalized and organic experiences
delivered by "Mom" will create unforgettable
memories for customers.

3 **Identify your own singular rock stars**—
depending on your business's particular
needs, consider the type of mold you are
trying to fill before hiring. Just remember:
unique people create unique experiences.

I read a headline that said the age of the rock star is dead, but it looks pretty alive to me.

MACHINE GUN KELLY

ROCK STARS
ARE THE
EXPERIENCE

WHEN IT comes down to it, the true differentiator for a sustainable business is service. However, the unforgettable service experience you want for your customers will not come from a product or initiative; it will happen because of a person. Especially if my definition of company culture rings true—that it is, at the core, a collection of individual human behaviors—then, logically, a great customer service culture is only possible with great service-minded individuals.

THE KEY TO CONSUMER LOYALTY

My business partner Brant Menswar and I have had many experiences at a local Denny's diner and a BurgerFi where the server or cashier not only remembers us but perfectly recalls our customized orders, sometimes several months between visits. That type of cognizant personalization matters to us and influences us to keep going back.

The employee empowered to provide unparalleled experiences is the key to creating consumer loyalty. Loyalty ensures repeat business, which in turn ensures ongoing, profitable growth for the company. As a believer in this "service-profit chain," you *must* start with employees to trigger this domino effect. We are loyal because of the person, not the product.

But employees (and customers) are a bit different these days, aren't they?

THE DECLINE ON BOTH SIDES

The general public knows great customer service has sadly been whittled away over the years. People say it to me personally, they validate it in focus groups and it's blatantly clear in industry surveys... service that rocks is as rare as Prince having appeared on a talk show. You most likely have concluded the same based on your own experiences; you don't need a detailed report to prove it. It's a transparent problem everywhere.

The average person may blame the overall service decline on a lack of employee training or the "way kids are brought up today," but in any case, they are smart enough to realize that the problem isn't with a process; it's with the human beings who fulfill it.

Sadly, customers aren't any better. The stage was already set in the U.S. with political divisiveness, racial unrest and cancel culture, but once the world's population experienced the collective trauma of COVID-19 and the global pandemic, decades of pent-up angst and frustration turned into anger and vitriol. The sheer rudeness of customers is now on par with the rampant apathy of many employees and has created a frustrating confluence of events. But you can't control customers; you can only change their hearts and minds by consistently bringing something spectacular to the party. That only happens through rock star employees.

Luckily, that is something you *do* have some influence over.

DIFFERENTIATION AS A SACRED MANTRA

Creating memorable experiences is the ultimate goal for lifestyle brands like Harley-Davidson, Red Bull and Patagonia, but now it has become every service-oriented business's sacred mantra. And in today's environment, it's the one that really matters.

If you want to deliver service that rocks, you're going to have to think and approach it differently.

KICK-ASS SERVICE

How you get to the point of competitor domination is what separates the good from the great. And this is again going to rely on human beings. Becoming a rock icon, rather than a one-hit wonder, starts with ensuring that you have the right talent delivering the right service.

The common theme is simple: the deliverer matters most.

Hard Rock International took the business-critical concept of "the deliverer matters most" and created a detailed and branded service philosophy around it to ensure that every team member on the planet both understood it and delivered it when dealing with customers. It was initially called "Kick-Ass Service" (perfect for the irreverent brand), but eventually morphed into the safe but appropriately named "Amplified Service." Regardless of the name, the specific approach was as crystal clear as Chris Cornell's voice.

These simple steps for an employee could be the basis of any customer service philosophy for companies looking to differentiate themselves:

1 Read the customer.
2 Seize the moment.
3 Personalize the experience.

Simple, but powerful. If every employee knew that their main function was to identify what it would require, at that moment, with that specific customer to completely rock their world—whether it was subtle or over-the-top—how could you not produce herculean results?

Brian Austin + the Wine Islands

One of my favorite disciples of Kick-Ass Service was Brian Austin, a stellar bartender at the Hard Rock Hotel's branded Velvet Bar. Brian was a true rocker: visible tattoos, multiple piercings, a beard that rivalled those of ZZ Top, a fun and irreverent attitude and a super quick approach to everything he did. Among all those qualities, Brian also displayed amazing attention to detail.

One night, a patron who was attending a conference was in the bar drinking red wine while wearing a white blazer. You know where this is going, right? Sure enough, at some point, the guest spilled the wine on his own expensive jacket and was visibly upset about ruining the outfit. Without skipping a beat, Brian pointed out the spill and loudly said, "Hey, that looks like the Wine Islands," as the spill actually looked like an island formation. If that wasn't funny and potentially off-putting enough, Brian asked the guest if he could take the jacket home for the night to see if he could do something with it; an odd request, which the patron agreed to, since the jacket seemed to be ruined anyway.

Brian took the jacket home and drew bold borders around the stains, along with the words "Wine Islands," and literally bedazzled the jacket with sequins as a designed masterpiece. When he presented it to the hotel guest the following night, the patron was so blown away with Brian's wit and ingenuity that he gave him a $100 tip and a huge thank-you for turning his ruined blazer into a rock star showpiece... which he proudly wore the rest of the night.

Brian Austin *is* the experience.

Lily + the Greatest Cup of Coffee

The National Restaurant Association touts that the majority of people in the United States will work at some point in the food service industry, many of them as their first job, developing their first real skills in serving others. If a frontline employee has an engrained hospitality gene or an authentic disposition to please others, they will surely succeed. Whether you have worked in the industry before or you're just a lover of eating and drinking at establishments, I'm sure many of your rock star experiences have revolved around food or drinks.

During his keynote speeches, and in a recorded online video that now boasts over two million views, sales and leadership expert Ryan Estis shares a story of being stranded in an airport on Christmas Eve, already depressed by some horrific news regarding his parents' health, yet he had his world completely rocked (positively) by a coffee barista named Lily.

The authentic and personable service that Lily delivered to everyone she came into contact with was so refreshing that it transcended the usual product transaction at an airport. In fact, the discussion between Lily and Ryan wasn't about providing a cup of coffee for customers. Lily enacted her mission to pour "happiness into people's lives." Knowing how tough air travel is, especially during the holidays, Lily volunteered to work on Christmas with the explicit goal to provide happiness to as many people as she could. Like Springsteen delivering a 3.5-hour, no-break, sweat-soaked marathon every single performance, Lily decides every day to "show up," give her best self to everyone and create moments that rock.

Ryan Estis proudly professes that he will never forget that cup of coffee for the rest of his life. And it has nothing to do with the coffee.

Lily *is* the experience.

Jeff, the Piano Man

I recently helped a friend move from a large house into a much smaller townhome. Between the two of us, we did a pretty good job of boxing, lifting and transporting 90 percent of everything in the house. But when it came to large, heavy items—piano, couches, entertainment centers, treadmill, and so on—we left that to the professionals.

My friend had arranged for a local moving company that specializes in moving pianos to come by with two personnel to handle the final items. One of the helpers was a Gen Z college student who was making a little extra money on the weekends. The other mover, Jeff, was a real go-getter and made this traditionally mundane experience a sight to behold.

Jeff was several decades older than his young partner and, although he was in great shape from all the daily furniture lifting, had some real "wear and tear" on him. He looked like he had been doing this for a long time. But watching him work was amazing.

Like Eddie Van Halen shredding on guitar, Jeff moved at blazing speed—faster than any furniture mover I had ever seen—and seemed to transport five times as many items to the truck as his co-worker.

During all his brisk movements, Jeff never hit any walls or scuffed any furniture. And all the while, he smiled from ear to ear, never complained about anything and was as respectful as any corporate business leader.

After the truck was loaded, we had a candid conversation about his work ethic and cheerful disposition, which rocked my world knowing that he genuinely loved his job and looked forward to each customer's move. And it showed. I honestly felt like this guy could work in any industry, but he *chose* to do this work— this tiring and demanding work—to make people's transitions in life better.

Now, every time I see a furniture moving crew trucking down the road, I think about Jeff… and what *could* be possible in that line of work. We need more Jeffs in the world.

Jeff *is* the experience.

Brian, Lily and Jeff are total rock stars. In their own way, each one of them proves, once again, that the product or the industry doesn't matter; it's the experience delivered by a person that makes the difference. The deliverer matters most.

And we are better served because of them.

GREATEST HITS

1 **Implement the service-profit chain**—to
create customer loyalty and bottom-line
results, focus predominantly on hiring and
retaining employees who are empowered
to provide unparalleled experiences. The
deliverer matters most.

2 **Think "different"**—to create memorable
experiences for today's customers, consider
employing some different approaches—
perhaps a bit more personal, irreverent and
unpredictable than usual.

3 **Create a service philosophy**—implement
a simple customer service philosophy with
memorable steps that all employees could
implement, practically guaranteeing positive
experiences: Read the Customer, Seize the
Moment, Personalize the Experience.

Music is forever;
music should grow
and mature with you,
following you right on
up until you die.

PAUL SIMON

SERVICE AT THE END OF THE LINE

T O DIVE DEEPER into customer service and demonstrate how strong service practices can positively affect business success, I am highlighting the cultural change possibilities in some industries, some of which could not be further from my background.

DEATH CARE THAT ROCKS?

I have been fortunate enough to be invited to speak on the topic of customer service at a variety of conferences. Surprisingly, some of my biggest clients are funeral directors. A good percentage of my sessions over the years have been in the funeral industry—or "death care," as it is sometimes called. Unless you currently work in that field, your initial reaction is probably what I hear all the time: "Seriously? What possibly could the spiky-haired, former Hard Rock guy talk about with funeral directors?"

My answer: the same things I talk about with every other profession—culture, service, engagement and leadership. These crucial subjects matter just as much in the funeral industry as they do to restaurants, retail and hotels.

On the surface, it seems like an unlikely pairing; the two universes of hospitality and death care appear as polar opposite as Taylor Swift and Kanye West. But the hopes and desires of these two business worlds are more alike than you would think.

TAKING A CUE FROM HOSPITALITY

As in any other service-oriented industry, funeral homes are highly competitive. Business owners in this field are constantly searching for ways to differentiate themselves from the competition. Although this is a generalization about the industry, the majority of the funeral directors who hired me or responded well to my message were looking for an outside-the-industry perspective on how to enhance their service culture. It may have been that I was just a catalyst through which their networking groups could address other challenges, but customer service differentiation is among my "most requested hits."

My impression, now based on conversations with
literally hundreds of funeral professionals, is that the
industry had focused for so long on the product—
caskets, urns, burial vaults and plots—that the
service proposition had become rigid, formalized and
predictable. Perhaps that is exactly what families want
in a funeral service, as there are no perfect guidelines
on how to deal with the loss of a loved one. And yet,
when I think about today's generation, I wonder how
they would like to honor, revere or celebrate a loss.

In my quest to bring something different to
the death care industry, I encouraged funeral
directors to take a cue from hospitality. Assuming
the role of thought-starter, I lobbied on just about
everything from physical infrastructure to alternative
entertainment, with the hope some businesses would
break out of their long-standing tradition of doing
things the same way.

Consider a few of the best practices I present to
funeral home directors when I facilitate sessions
with them.

Blow Out the Building Design

When it comes to the actual design of a funeral home, I propose oversized furniture in the lobby and sitting rooms to offer families—their clients—more comfort. I've suggested "raising the roof," versus sticking with the typical low ceilings I have experienced, to help alleviate some of the sadness that may be accentuated by a pressure-filled enclosed space. And since visual backdrops have become more and more common in indoor services, laptops, built-in LCD projectors and screens are must-haves for families wanting to show a PowerPoint slideshow of pictures, quotes, music lyrics or scripture verses.

Amp Up the Music Offering

Because music is a critical part of the current generation's lifestyle, this is an area where corners simply cannot be cut. Great sound systems—not the crackly speakers originally built into the ceiling—should be a part of the viewing or service rooms. The system should include state-of-the-art speakers, quality microphones, great WiFi and a sound chord jack (or Bluetooth system) to plug into the client's smartphone, allowing families to customize the experience with their own playlists. Funeral homes should also provide contact information for local musicians as an option for those who want live music but do not have a personal resource.

Create Hospitality Events

We live in an era in which many families remember their loved ones by *celebrating* their lives. Consider setting up the event to reflect the individual. Many services now resemble hospitality events: guitars might be used as decorations on the buffet line; music CDs might be repurposed as food item labels; the loved one's Harley-Davidson motorcycle might even be parked inside the funeral home as part of the experience. Whether the funeral is "themed" around music, sports, motorcycles or something else, funeral directors should recognize that families often want— and appreciate—the option to create a personalized event to commemorate the passing of a loved one. Funeral directors should alter their service practices to better reflect this shift in family expectations.

Consider Today's Generational Mind

Today's younger generation is more socially conscious than ever. Its members actively seek out ways to leave a smaller footprint in the world. Using recycled materials wherever possible will be noticed and appreciated, but cremation and possibly even safe, biodegradable caskets could be options as well.

A funeral home should always be a reflection of its clients, offering various avenues and mediums to achieve whatever result a family desires.

EVEN IN MOMENTS OF DESPAIR

Some funeral directors may be resistant to using these specific approaches in their companies, fearing that doing so will cut into their profit margins, alienate them from families that desire more traditional experiences or be overwhelmingly difficult to execute. But having the ability to offer clients diverse options and a customized experience will certainly help put their business into a family's mental shelf space for when a need arises in the future. People remember the unique, even in moments of despair. The more you can personalize or customize the experience for the family, the more unforgettable the company. This is a tenet for any service-oriented brand.

THE MORE YOU CAN PERSONALIZE THE EXPERIENCE, THE MORE UNFORGETTABLE THE COMPANY.

———

TAKING IT TO THE NEXT LEVEL

I do not personally know of any funeral organizations that have adopted *all* the ideas I have mentioned, but a few have implemented some, many later sharing with me the success stories resulting from the time we spent together. One funeral home now *always* offers a local bagpipe player as a nice touch for the service. Another funeral director *always* provides personalized Starbucks coffee drinks to the immediate family at the viewing, knowing a warm cup of coffee is comforting during the process. Yet another owner even created a supervised children's area in the funeral home, complete with quiet games, to allow the adults to focus on the visitation in the next room without the distraction of active children.

During a networking session, one professional confessed that he had been pretty determined *not* to implement change in his services over the years... until he sat through my program on customer service. Shortly afterward, a client requested that he allow family members to dip their hands in paint and place their palm prints directly onto the loved one's casket before lowering it into the ground. After some contemplation, he decided to honor the request.

This funeral director later confided that he would not have endorsed this idea in the past, but since my presentation he had become more willing to personalize the experience he offered. He now offers this option to everyone who uses his business.

A few funeral directors have told me that they now do services and events with ice sculptures as part of the experience. One funeral home in California uses a customized Hummer instead of a hearse to transport bodies to their final resting place. That one blew my mind.

But the one who takes home the gold record for "Most Creative Innovation" in his service practices is the funeral director who installed an Icee machine at his funeral home. Just like the children's area at another business, this slushy frozen treat was the business owner's approach to entertaining the kids while the adults made funeral arrangements close by. He freely admits the machine is time-consuming and the messiest piece of equipment he has ever dealt with, yet the unspoken comfort the families feel when the children are occupied while the adults make tough emotional decisions is well worth the daily maintenance. He even told me that families now occasionally stop by the funeral home for free Icees— which he is perfectly content to accommodate because he knows that when there is a loss in the family, his is the phone they will ring.

These business operators are reaching higher; they're undertaking (no pun intended) a constant journey to improve, reinvent and enhance their service practices.

These are culture catalysts who have created a point of differentiation, even in the way we honor death.

Death care is just one industry on a mission to differentiate itself from the rest to survive and even thrive. You may not initially think of your industry as hospitality-oriented, but we can all take a cue from brands that use serving people as their platform for success.

GREATEST HITS

1 Transcend your industry service standards—
regardless of industry or location, serious
business leaders understand, covet and insist
on the crucial key tenet of great customer
service to create true differentiation.

2 Think unique—people remember the unique,
even in moments of despair. The more you
can personalize or customize the experience
for your specific customers, the more
unforgettable the company.

3 Go on the never-ending quest—culture
catalysts are on a constant journey to
improve, reinvent and amp up their service
practices (even in the way we honor death).

I'm experimental by nature... always exploring my creativity.

CHRISTINA AGUILERA

TAKING PAGES FROM OTHER SONGBOOKS

L IKE THE experiential steps of funeral directors, other industries are starting to pay attention to the overall customer experience and not just hang their hat on the product or the environment. Thankfully, health care is one of those industries.

RESUSCITATING HEALTH CARE

As proof of the shift in health care, hospitals are hiring executives from the hospitality sector. During a recruiting presentation at a local conference I attended, the speaker shared some data from the University of Florida showing that major hospitals were leaning more and more toward applicants who had hospitality experience on their resumé. It didn't guarantee them the job, but when they were matched up against another similarly qualified candidate, the one who had worked in a restaurant or hotel had the upper hand in landing the gig.

Let me share a few examples of how experience in a customer-obsessed service culture can help out in any industry—especially health care.

Henry Ford Health System, Detroit

In May 2011, Jessica Watson published an article in Henry Ford's online newsletter about Sven Gierlinger's appointment as vice president of Customer Hospitality and Service Culture for the Detroit-based company. This was a newly created position.

I was amazed to discover that Gierlinger's background included more than twenty years of experience in hospitality, including a stint as vice president of Museum Operations at the Detroit Institute of Arts, one of the nation's top art museums. His accomplishments included coordinating a $158-million renovation of the museum and implementing a comprehensive customer service initiative that changed the workforce culture.

While working in the hospitality industry, Gierlinger opened six hotels in four countries in nine years, including Ritz-Carlton properties in the United States, Germany, Japan and Indonesia. He also holds a bachelor's degree in hotel business administration from the Bavaria Hotel Management School in Germany. So... some serious hospitality cred.

Is there any doubt about the reason he was chosen by this Detroit health care organization? The Henry Ford Health System was on the hunt for a service culture makeover.

Columbia Asia Hospital, India

In February 2011, the *Economic Times*, a non–industry specific, international media outlet for the world's economic news, featured an article detailing the appointment of Tufan Ghosh as CEO at Columbia Asia Hospitals in Bangalore, India. The co-authors specifically noted that Ghosh was making this transition after working fifteen years with the Oberoi Group, a global chain of premium hotels and resorts that has been voted many times over as "The World's Leading Luxury Hotel Brand." You can imagine that the change of scenery was radical for Ghosh. But that was precisely why he was hired. Ghosh was an expert in the field of hospitality—and, like Elvis busting onto the rock and roll scene, health care needed a radical infusion of hospitality.

HEALTH CARE'S MAKEOVER

Hospitals no longer want to be seen as tiresome rows of patient-care wards. As medical tourism becomes popular and competition among private hospitals heats up, these businesses are hiring executives from the hospitality sector. As was reported in the *Economic Times*, most people surveyed in India claimed not to use public health facilities, mostly because of their apprehensions about the quality of care, lack of accessibility, long waiting times and generally poor experiences. To ensure customer loyalty, innovative companies like Columbia Asia recognized the need to go the extra mile and provide personalized attention and care. To address this very issue, many of the executives in this hospital group were hired from the hotel industry.

In October 2010, Shannon Kraus wrote an online article for *Healthcare Design Magazine* focusing on the industry's initiatives to reimagine the patient/family experience, from building design to customer-focused care. Kraus reported that intertwining hospitality design with health care architecture is not a new concept. For more than a decade, health care architects have been using hospitality-like finishes to create destination-type settings that connect with their communities while appealing to patients. Super comfortable beds, fluffy bedspreads, warm wood flooring, balconies attached to rooms, soothing colors and pictures on patient room walls, music wafting through the corridors, meditation areas and gardens located throughout health pavilions are all part of this image makeover.

Lancaster General Hospital, Pennsylvania

In that same article, Kraus also shared a great case study about a hospital in Lancaster, Pennsylvania, that had a clear mission when it planned its facility on a seventy-acre site: "To create an extraordinary experience every time."

What? An "extraordinary experience" in a hospital? Yep, that was the goal.

So, the hospitality design approach was incorporated into every aspect of the project, creating more of a "life campus" than a hospital. The owner and design team visualized a "guest" room with health amenities, rather than a simple patient room. They envisioned waiting rooms as living rooms; the cafeteria as a restaurant-style dining area; a kitchen that could provide tasty, diet-friendly menus; a farmers market to introduce fresh produce to the campus. One of the central themes of the whole life campus is that it should be a place where people would come when they were healthy. But as you know by now, even all of that isn't enough.

PATIENTS AS ROCK ROYALTY

Today, a new wave of health care facilities is considering the patient experience beyond just the rooms. The innovative design approach views the patient as a "guest" first—creating a new, implied personal contract. While patients are something to be processed, guests are to be treated like rock royalty. So, the idea of guest-focused care is about getting into the DNA of design and introducing attitudes that focus on the guest experience. The result is the renewed approach of "hospitality meets health care design" that goes further than it ever has in the past.

Surveys, such as those conducted by Hospital Consumer Assessment of Healthcare Providers and Systems, have shown that hospitals incorporating extra features and amenities score higher in satisfaction. But guest-focused care is about supporting the *experience* with the design. It's about creating a hospitality mindset. One of the first lessons in hospitality design is that 90 percent of what establishes the difference between a two-star hotel and a five-star hotel is service—not the building or the amenities.

True, the environment is always critical, but it only sets the stage for the performer to rock people's worlds. The goal is to go beyond the physical product and instead focus predominantly on the service being delivered. It is only then that the hospital experience can be redefined from being short-term, patient-focused care to being holistic guest-focused care, raising the bar for health care delivery.

FORCES OF MAGNETISM

As many health care facility operators know, the key driver today is patient satisfaction. Satisfied patients lead to improved market share, since most consumers choose their providers. They are also more likely to recommend a facility to friends or family. And now they are keeping score.

Hospital businesses have created scorecards that rank items from patient satisfaction to hospital outcomes and performance. Many of these are made public and are tracked in public forums. While this may be controversial in the health care industry, it is indicative of health care's increased accountability to the consumer.

In 1990, the American Nurses Credentialing Center created "The Magnet Recognition Program" to recognize health care organizations for quality patient care, nursing excellence and innovations in professional nursing practice. Achieving Magnet status is a big deal. The designation is only awarded to hospitals that embody the highest service cultures. Amazingly, this once self-designated award created by health care employees to raise the bar in patient care has now become an industry standard. Consumers now rely on the Magnet designation as *the* ultimate credential for high-quality nursing.

In these elite health care systems:

- There is no need to advertise for open positions; there are plenty of high-quality candidates-in-waiting.

- Contract nurses are not needed; full-time nursing teams are staffed 100 percent of the time.

- Doctors value all nurses on the team; everyone is perceived and treated with equal respect.

- Teams have development improvement plans, used regularly to seek continuous improvement.

- Nurses write and publish research papers, many on critical topics leading to financial impact.

- Magnet pins—envied and sought after by all in the industry—are awarded to all the staff.

To apply for Magnet status, hospitals must provide detailed proof of their culture of communication, teamwork, patient service and supporting values. To even be considered, a health care system must provide all-inclusive data from the previous three years. Once attained, Magnet status has a very positive impact on turnover and team engagement.

Lancaster General Hospital, mentioned earlier, has been one of these Magnet systems for several years, which makes sense, given their quest "to create an extraordinary experience every time."

In every industry, the overall service experience matters—now more than ever. As much as I may *like* a product, the service experience is always going to be the clincher. As much as I may *need* a product, the service experience is always going to make it better.

Let me give you another example.

ONE OF LIFE'S GREAT FINDS

Think about the automotive repair industry and your personal experiences having cars fixed. Anyone who owns a vehicle must go through this ritual multiple times, perhaps even several times a year, depending on the quality of the car, your ongoing proactive maintenance of the vehicle and your propensity for getting into accidents. You might put a car in the shop for something as small and relatively inexpensive as an oil change or tire alignment, or something as big and wallet-busting as a transmission repair or air conditioning unit replacement. It's a business that will be desperately needed for as long as we continue to use complicated driving machines that require expertise to keep them going.

A repair shop that employs skilled mechanics and sets a fair price is one of life's greatest finds for a vehicle owner. Yet the rare, differentiating ingredient of great service tends to be absent from many automotive brands, necessitating our ongoing quest for the perfect mechanic. So the hunt continues.

As with the funeral industry, my experience with auto repair business owners suggests that they also see their company as a product-oriented business. It is not. Most vehicle maintenance companies have not fully realized that their business is a service, with "fixing a vehicle" as the by-product. The means to this end matters. It may not be as important for some of the older, more loyal customers enjoyed by *some* auto shops, but that clientele is quickly transitioning to the experience-starved consumers of the twenty-first century—and they require a bit more.

MY EXPERIENCE IS IN THE SHOP

I would bet that the general driving public has had similar experiences and, therefore, shares my mindset: *nobody* wants to put their vehicle in the shop and *everybody* is going to be frustrated with the extent of the problem and the cost of the repair.

Isn't it possible to change that perception, if the experience is positive and the value proposition is high?

No doubt the repair work has to be done regardless, and customers may not ever look forward to this inevitable disruption, but the overall experience can still be dramatically altered to make auto repair more palatable. I believe the service delivery alone could be so mind-blowing that it might even become shockingly enjoyable. I can easily imagine the numerous physical plant changes one could make to the repair shop itself, especially the waiting room, just to offset the hassle and disruption brought on by car trouble. In my mind's eye, when I think about a revolutionized vehicle maintenance waiting area, I envision a hotel lobby:

- Free premium and fair-trade coffee available— Lavazza, Green Mountain, Gevalia and so on

- Self-serve containers of fruit-infused ice water— lemon, pineapple, melon and so on

- Free WiFi

- Comfortable furniture with a mix of ergonomic and overstuffed seating

- An abundance of power outlets with easy access for laptops and phone charging

- Flat-screen televisions, versus an older, bulky unit sitting on a cart

- Warm paint colors on the wall

- Potted plants in the corners

- Recessed and directional lighting that, along with the paint and plants, softens the room

- A chalk wall for kids to draw on
- Up-to-date newspapers and magazines available, including inexpensive subscriptions like *USA Today*, *Rolling Stone* and so on
- Immaculate restrooms

Certainly there are some upfront capital costs here, but I would look at this as an investment likely to gain an immediate financial return in the form of loyal customers—new clients and regulars alike. Instead of dropping the car off and then running to a more pleasing "staging" area away from the shop, I would feel like staying in this type of space. And although an enhanced atmosphere like this would still not be enough to guarantee my return, a premium, customer-focused environment would definitely lay the groundwork for a more value-oriented service experience.

To truly make a lasting impression and secure financial sustainability, an emotional experience needs to occur for the consumer.

REIMAGINING AUTO REPAIR

How can an automotive repair business create a "Wow!" moment for customers?

The same way everyone else can: surprise and delight them with some value-added moments of differentiation. Consider what would happen if an automotive repair shop did the following for free... for *every* customer:

- Emerged from behind the service counter to offer a personable greeting—perhaps even a handshake—versus the traditional "How can I help you?"

- Cleaned the automobile dashboard

- Washed the windows inside and out

- Vacuumed the floor mats

- Topped off the windshield wiper fluid

- Placed a handwritten thank-you card on the passenger seat

- Gave an inexpensive gift, like a mini-flashlight, calendar, pen—even a lollipop for kids

- Sent a birthday card to the customer on their special day

I'm sure there are many people who think these suggestions go *way* too far or that these types of perks should be reserved for high-paying, VIP members, not some random customer who came in for the discounted oil change that was advertised on the side of the road. But I think just the opposite. Vehicle maintenance shops should look for opportunities to stand out from the crowd and rock the world of every customer, regardless of the work provided. A shop owner wouldn't have to implement *all* of the ideas on the list—just enough of them to differentiate themselves. Without these kinds of service extras, the business will always be looked at as a commodity, and consumers will base their decision to come back on the price of the product alone.

It's not enough. People want more.

PERSONALIZED SERVICE WINS EVERY TIME

In the past two chapters, you have seen some unique and interesting examples of outside-the-box service. These companies diligently and meticulously work to ensure that they are the chocolate in a world full of vanilla. They spend valuable resources like time and money to evaluate and understand their potential customers so they can tap into their true wants and desires.

In fact, these "monsters of rock" examples are the places—with the types of people—in which I like to spend my money. I imagine that the same is true for you. We helplessly hunger to be surprised by spectacular service, mostly because the great majority of companies simply do not feed our appetites. It's why we happily pay to go see P!nk, Lady Gaga or Silk Sonic; we know the value experienced far exceeds the cost of the show.

All the companies I mentioned have created a service culture to be envied by others. Even if the memory was initially tied to a thing or a process, like hospital room amenities or an Icee machine in a funeral home, the overall experience still had to be supported by positive interactions with employees.

SERVICE TRUMPS PRODUCT, PRICE, CONVENIENCE AND THEME— EVERY TIME.

———

People who make a living in a service-oriented business will agree that out of everything they do, providing memorable customer service makes the only real difference between success and failure. This continues to be validated by countless studies and industry associations dedicated to measuring and assessing this service-to-sustainable-success correlation. But even if you didn't have access to or knowledge of these expert results as proof, you already know it to be true. Even the average customer knows that great service—especially personalized service—is much more important than anything else.

In other words, service trumps product, price, convenience and theme.

Always has. Always will.

GREATEST HITS

1 **Let rock stars perform**—although the environment is always critical, it is only the stage set for the performer to rock people's worlds. The goal is to go beyond the physical product and focus predominantly on the service being delivered.

2 **Let the experience shine**—many people see their company as a product-oriented business, but it is not. Smart leaders realize that their business is an experience, with the product as part of the price of admission.

3 **Know that service trumps product, price, convenience and theme every time**—providing memorable customer service makes the only real difference between success and failure.

You've got to try and take things to the next level, or you'll just get stuck in a rut.

OZZY OSBOURNE

BEYOND THE PRICE OF ADMISSION

PEOPLE LOVE to be positively surprised. It makes consumers feel like they're special. Many of the memorable examples I share all include elements of unpredictability—they were completely and utterly unexpected by the customer. And those are the moments worth sharing. When you consider your service practices, focus a great deal of attention on your ability to surprise and delight a customer, whether planned or organic.

To be a competitive business, you must constantly separate yourself from the rest of your industry by being an innovator. The choice is yours. But if your customers leave your business with a welcomed sense of astonishment and revelation, they will also leave with a desire to return, if for no other reason than to see what other magic tricks you have up your sleeve.

UNPREDICTABILITY CAN BE COOL

Of course, customers have certain preconceived expectations of what they are going to get with a business, but creating some mystery or delight of the unanticipated should be considered. This is what makes artists like Madonna so great, or what made Bowie legendary. It's not just the music, or the sets, or the costumes; it's also the unpredictable moments they spring on us that put us over the edge. Let's explore this.

How do you think a customer would react if you or one of your employees were to surprise them with something unexpected? For example:

- What would happen if a call center employee impulsively offered to pay for a customer's shipping costs? Not because something was going wrong, but because the employee recognized the importance of delighting a regular and valued consumer. Would the employee be reprimanded or celebrated?

- What would happen if a bartender noticed a returning guest—one who was at the bar for the first time the night before—and decided to make him a drink "on the house" as a way of saying thank you for the patronage? What do you suppose the customer would say about the place after he left?

- How do you think a receiving clerk would respond to getting an order delivered from a box company in which the sales representative has surprisingly thrown in an extra supply of free boxes and a kind note, just to solidify the relationship?

- What would a homeowner do if a lawn fertilizer company noticed that her yard needed some big-time care, compared to the neighbors, and stopped by to offer her a free, no-strings-attached fertilizer spray, just to keep her in the good graces of the neighborhood?

These unexpected moments are the types of subtle techniques that smart individuals use to stoke the relationship fire between brand and customer. Of course, not every idea has to cost money. There are also little-to-no-cost experiences just waiting to be created. For example:

- How would a customer feel about getting a personalized birthday card from his auto insurance agent (even if it was an electronic card via email)— not with the intent to sell more policies, but purely to create an unexpected memory and keep their relationship front and center?

- How do you think a person would feel if her hairdresser said he loved her new look so much that he wanted to take a picture of the stylish cut and post it on his Instagram page? Don't you think she would be on cloud nine over this type of attention?

- How do you think a homeowner would feel if they discovered that a real estate agent had left a door hanger on the front door that said, "Your home is incredible! Out of all the houses in this neighborhood, yours is the only one I left this note on. If you ever decide to sell, you deserve a rock star real estate agent." Other than the initial ego stroke for the homeowner, don't you think this agent now has an opportunity to represent this house's sale in the future?

- What would happen if an airline ticket agent noticed a passenger wearing a baseball team jersey and commented positively about his favorite team, even reaching out to give him a high five? How would that passenger feel about that unexpected moment over a shared love of a sports team?

- How would a customer feel if her local print company, in an impromptu tweet to all of the company's Twitter fans, singled her out to say how much they appreciated her?

I hope these examples of unpredictability help to get the juices flowing in your own mind, as you think about how you can create differentiation between your brand and the competition. To echo my earlier point, *not* knowing exactly what's going to happen to a customer in your business *could* be part of the experience.

Unpredictability is cool. It's refreshing. It's exciting. And it gets rewarded.

It isn't the *only* way to create memories, but surprising and delighting your customers is a great no-brainer to make your company stand out from the rest.

UNPREDICT-ABILITY IS COOL AND EXCITING— AND GETS REWARDED.

——

ADMONISH OR CELEBRATE?

Can an empowered employee in your organization avoid being rude and disrespectful while skirting the edge of irreverence—and be internally celebrated for it? For example:

- Would there be any harm if a sunglasses sales associate at a mall kiosk noticed an approaching shopper with a cowboy hat on and said, "What's up, Tex?" Are you too unsure of how someone might take that greeting?

- What would happen if a cable company employee answered the phone, "How can I rock your world?" Would you be too scared of how the customer might actually respond to that?

- How would guests at a theme park respond if, when they asked a tour guide to take a picture of them, that park employee turned the camera around and took a selfie, adding himself to their vacation pictures? Of course, in today's era of digital photography, many people would just delete the picture, no harm done—but *some* would keep the shot as a captured unforgettable moment of the overall experience. Would you discipline the employee or quietly celebrate his moxie?

EXPERIENTIAL OWNERSHIP

Even if the ideas I have shared in this chapter seem radical for your company, you can still cultivate a spirit of "experiential ownership" in your team. That is, if the end goal is to turn your customers into raving fans, then empowering your employees to make memory-searing moments—as if *they* were the business owners—should be relished and celebrated. When your staff takes ownership in creating authentic, unforgettable experiences for clients, they will be inspired to do more. The customers will love the memories they forge, and employees will be jazzed to create them. If we really do hire for attitude, as many of us claim to, then let's get out of the way and let our employees use that attitude to wow our customers.

This idea may still shock many executives and human resource professionals who fear that it will result in an employee counseling session, a customer complaint or, even worse, a lawsuit. But deep down inside, those same company professionals know "right fit" employees are the ones who make a real difference in company culture and drive an organization's sustainable future.

Remember, unique people create unique experiences.

Jellyfish

I had a fantastic service experience happen to me while I was helping open a business in the Dominican Republic. On one of our free nights, the new management team took the director of operations and me to dinner at a local outdoor restaurant called Jellyfish. The fresh seafood was spectacular, the scenery was picturesque and the conversations were great— but it was the music that really made it a memorable evening for me.

When we first walked in, typical Caribbean music was playing in the background for the six to eight different parties already seated. About halfway through our meal, however, I noticed a switch from local reggae, merengue and bachata music to the more familiar classic rock tunes I love—now playing prominently in the foreground. At the end of our table, my friend Tom Perez and I lost ourselves in the journey back to the 60s and 70s, singing along to every tune.

When I asked the restaurant manager what radio station was playing so I could tune in during my stay on the island, his response took me aback. He said it was not a traditional Dominican radio station, but rather the music was coming through a satellite radio he'd installed a few months earlier, just for an occasion like this. He had noticed when I walked in that I was an American, and he had perfectly selected the right time to switch the station to classic rock, making the music an organic part of the experience—specifically for me.

Wow. Talk about someone who is motivated to customize an experience to his clientele. Too cool. Of course, the enjoyable environment compelled us to stay for desserts and coffee, which didn't hurt his business either.

Regardless of your business, look for ways to personalize the experience for your consumers, like this restaurant manager did for me—and don't be afraid to go for it. When the service experience moves from a traditional business process to one that is thoughtfully catered to the individual, the customer will remember it forever. You can expect guests not only to come back and spend more money but also to tell everyone they know about you. And those are the three most important metrics in any business.

Mission BBQ

Christy Cox, VP of human resources for Twice Daily, a Tennessee-based convenience store chain, told me about traveling to her cousin's funeral during the global pandemic. The family came to the service from all over the U.S. and eventually met afterward at a Mission BBQ location in Virginia.

Mission BBQ opened its doors on September 11, 2010—nine years after our world was changed forever. The patriotic founders of this company operate with a servant's heart and use barbecue as the platform to give back to heroes—those who serve others—but also with a specific "mission" to make people's lives better. As you can imagine, it is critical that the team members employed with this brand emphatically represent the company's values.

This Mission BBQ location's team did.

The restaurant effortlessly accommodated Christy's large group after the funeral and were attentive throughout the entire dining experience. Obviously aware of the reason for the gathering, at the end of the meal, the restaurant team sent out a complimentary basket of warm cookies for the whole table. The family truly appreciated it. If that wasn't enough, as the cookies were plucked from the basket, a handwritten message was revealed on the wax paper that lined the bottom of the basket, which read, "We're very sorry for your loss."

I mean...!

With one inexpensive and heartfelt gesture, this group of thoughtful humans created a moment Christy's family will never forget.

That is service that rocks.

Portofino Hotel

A friend of mine came to Orlando for a family vacation and stayed at the Portofino, a themed resort hotel located at Universal Studios' Citywalk and modeled after the famed bay resort in Italy. After a long day of playing at the theme parks, his family dropped all their purchased logo clothing, swag and merchandise in their room and went out for dinner. Upon returning to the room, his kids were completely stunned by what they discovered. The stuffed theme park characters they had bought during the day were now sitting in the bed, under the covers, sheets turned back, remote control "in hand"... watching the Cartoon Network on television. It was a real-life *Toy Story* moment for this family.

Can you just picture what the kids' faces looked like at that moment? Sheer astonishment and pure joy.

Obviously, an attentive housekeeper included this small but powerful gesture as part of the hotel's turndown service. But it blows my mind that this rock star would not even be present for the "shock and awe" moment the family would experience. And one they will never forget.

ATTENTIVE MEMORY MAKERS

When was the last time you returned to your hotel room to find stuffed animals in your bed watching television? Or a business owner catered the music specifically to you? Or you received free cookies and a handwritten note from a business as acknowledgment and comfort?

These examples are so rare and so far from the norm that customers are simply shocked when they occur. Maybe the better question is: Do you have stealth individuals like this working for your brand— employees who are on the hunt to create memorable moments for customers, even though some will not be present to witness the magic?

Unpredictable moments from attentive brand ambassadors, who have an insatiable desire to surprise and delight customers, are the legendary stories people will talk about the rest of their lives.

SHARE THE STORIES

Can you recall any unforgettable moments your brand has delivered, as a result of an employee's self-driven initiative to create an experience? I'm sure there are a few.

These stories need to be shared with everyone and celebrated in public. This will create an environment in which other team members will seize a moment to surprise the customer. Your employees need more choices in the songbook than just the same old standards—the traditional content taught in their training manuals. By capturing stories, like an employee's out-of-the-box initiative, as part of your ongoing service philosophy, your company's culture becomes stronger and more defined. It's these unique moments, generated by an individual, that differentiate your brand from the mediocre.

Share the stories. Foster their continuance. Enhance the culture.

GREATEST HITS

1 **Deliver unpredictability**—when you
consider your service practices, focus a
great deal of attention on your ability to
surprise and delight a customer, whether
planned or organic. Unpredictability is cool,
refreshing, exciting...and it gets rewarded.

2 **Choose the right "unique" for your culture**—
company professionals know "right fit"
employees are the ones who make a real
difference in company culture and drive an
organization's sustainable future.

3 **Cultivate experiential ownership**—to
turn customers into raving fans, empower
your employees to make memory-searing
moments—as if they were the business
owners. Then capture and share the stories.

ENCORE

WE HAVE covered a lot of ground in this book, but the core theme is the same throughout: a company's culture is enhanced by differentiated customer service. And when it is done right, the benefits for the brand are monumental. Small businesses and large corporations alike reap huge rewards from a great customer service culture.

BENEFITS OF A STRONG SERVICE CULTURE

Here are some of the unmistakable benefits that come from a well-defined and flawlessly executed customer service program:

- **Customers will return**—people only repeat what they like. When customers have an overwhelmingly positive experience, especially if it was personalized and customized for them, they will surely return for another dose of awesomeness.

- **You generate more revenue**—as happy customers continue to immerse themselves in an awesome company culture (based on employee behaviors), they will become loyal to your organization, not only coming back regularly and spending more money on your products and services, but becoming brand advocates by referring others to you as well.

- **You strengthen the bottom line**—this is the ultimate metric in most businesses: the bottom line of a profit and loss statement. Even in nonprofit volunteer organizations, a focus on the bottom line is critical. And profit is dependent on the overall customer experience.

- **You improve brand reputation**—the way your community views your company has the power to catapult you to higher sales, more and bigger donations, more media impressions and so on, ultimately creating a positive buzz about your business. That keeps customers talking positively about the company—especially using the power of social media. This self-fulfilling prophecy not only leads to returning customers but now influences others to take a peek at the brand.

Out of all the important tasks that company employees are responsible for, these outcomes are the only things that truly matter. Crush the overall experience and customers will come back, spend more and talk positively about the brand.

NEXT STEPS

Listen... delivering service that rocks is one of the hardest things you will ever do, because it requires employing humans with unique behaviors—some good, some not so good. But the work is worthwhile. And crucial to the brand's success.

To keep the fire going in your own quest to amplify your company's customer service approach, here are some immediate initiatives you can personally do:

- **Review the "Greatest Hits"**—as a holistic refresher, flip through this book again, paying particular attention to the "Greatest Hits" section at the end of each chapter. Look for opportunities to enhance the company's (or your own) service practices.

- **Share the book**—distribute copies of *Service That Rocks* to your team, who can also be catalysts, and collectively discuss how to amp up the customer experience.

- **Take the assessment**—download the free culture assessment at CultureThatRocks.com, which has several sections dedicated to customer service. This will provide an introspective gut check on where you, your team and your company are with service that rocks.

- **Get the series**—read the other books in the Culture That Rocks series—*Leadership That Rocks* (LeadershipThatRocksBook.com) and *Engagement That Rocks* (EngagementThatRocks.com), to keep learning about the big focal points of an iconic culture.

- **Pitch external expertise**—you may not be the ultimate decision maker, but recommending new customer service material and outside-the-box thinking from an external source is a great way to affect change, while also getting you noticed and advancing your career. (Psst ... I happen to know a speaker or two who can deliver in-person or virtual sessions for this exact strategy.)

Whatever industry you are in, the straightforward but powerful practices and stories I have shared will facilitate future growth and immeasurable success for your organization. When building the pillars that will define your organization in terms of direct service to customers, it is imperative that your foundation is anchored to choices and mechanisms that create a customer experience that will propel people back to your business time and time again.

Just remember: service trumps product, price, theme and convenience—every time.

That is *never* going to change.

I'm so honored that you made *Service That Rocks* a part of your journey and a resource in providing clear direction for how you can get customers to fall madly in love with your brand. You have both the power and the opportunity to be the measuring stick for all other companies in your industry. It just takes a little extra attention to service to take your company's culture to the next level.

Perhaps all the way up to eleven.

Rock On—

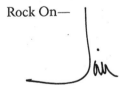

ACKNOWLEDGMENTS

BIG-TIME THANKS go to the following family, friends, businesses and mentors who each supported me in some way along the journey to craft *Service That Rocks*: my mom (Doris Knight), Kathleen Wood, Toni Quist, Brant Menswar, Monica Mattia, Michael and Tami Kneidinger, Laura Rolston, Karen Neeley Revels, Mike and Carol Shipley, Rich Johnson, Emily Ellis, Sheldon Suga, Christy Cox, Ron Tite, Ryan Estis, Janna Kiehl, Axum Coffee, Just Love Coffee, Foxtail Coffee, Hawks Cay Resort and the city of Winter Garden, Florida.

My sincerest gratitude goes to Page Two Books, who took a chance on me from day one and brought my vision to life. From the first discussion I had with Jesse Finkelstein to the ongoing guidance of the entire team, I always felt like I was in great hands. Rony and Adrineh kept me organized, Jenny and Crissy cleaned up my flaws, Peter made me look good and Chris and Madison helped me amplify my voice.

Finally, a huge thank-you goes to Kendra Ward, my amazing editor at Page Two, who is always a pure joy to work with. Kendra's personality and editorial style—the perfect balance between humility, patience, detail and expertise—helped me clarify my voice. Kendra is a total rock star!

PRODUCTS

CULTURE THAT ROCKS
How to Revolutionize a
Company's Culture
2014

**LEADERSHIP
THAT ROCKS**
**Take Your Brand's
Culture to Eleven and
Amp Up Results**
2021

SERVICE THAT ROCKS
Create Unforgettable
Experiences and Turn
Customers into Fans
2022

ENGAGEMENT
THAT ROCKS
Recruit and Retain
Chart-Topping Talent
2023

**LEADERSHIP THAT
ROCKS COMPANION
WORKBOOK**

CERTIFIED ROCK STAR
Facilitated leadership
training

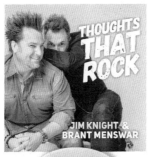

THOUGHTS THAT ROCK
Weekly leadership podcast

BOOKY CALL
Book discovery platform cleverly disguised as a dating app

ABOUT THE AUTHOR

JIM KNIGHT is an award-winning training and development veteran and culture catalyst who speaks on a variety of interactive topics, including programs on organizational culture, differentiated service, building rock star teams and leadership. During Jim's twenty-one-year career with Hard Rock International, his creativity and success garnered his team several industry awards for cutting-edge print, video, e-learning and instructor-led concepts. He was also recognized by *Training* magazine as representing one of the Training Top 125 companies in the world, across all industries, and has since been featured in *Entrepreneur* magazine, *Inc.* magazine, *Forbes* magazine and Fox Small Business News.

With a music degree in Vocal Performance and Education, a six-year stint as a public middle school teacher and his two decades with the Hard Rock brand, Jim uses all of his experience and expertise—

as a keynote speaker, podcaster, book marketer and author—to assist leaders of all levels and industries develop their skills and amp up business results.

Jim released his widely praised first book, *Culture That Rocks*, in 2014. It is now in its second edition—and is the impetus for *Service That Rocks*, book two in the Culture That Rocks series.

Jim also discusses life-changing leadership advice and best practices with influential guests on *Thoughts That Rock*, the free weekly edu-taining podcast that he co-hosts with Brant Menswar.

To contact Jim Knight, you can reach him at:

ServiceThatRocksBook.com

⊙ **@JimKnightSpeaker**

◐ **@KnightSpeaker**